Blackstone's G

DISABILITY DISCRIMINATION ACT 1995

Blackstone's Guide to the
DISABILITY DISCRIMINATION ACT 1995

Caroline Gooding LLM
(University of California of Berkeley)
Solicitor, Director of Disablity Law Service

**BLACKSTONE
PRESS LIMITED**

First published in Great Britain 1996 by Blackstone Press Limited,
9–15 Aldine Street, London W12 8AW. Telephone 0181-740 1173

© Caroline Gooding, 1996

ISBN: 1 85431 499 8

British Library Cataloguing in Publication Data
A CIP catalogue record for this book is available from the British Library.

Typeset by Montage Studios Limited, Tonbridge, Kent
Printed by Livesey Limited, Shrewsbury, Shropshire

Contents

Preface

The Disability Discrimination Act 1995 is the first British statute ever to address the issue of discrimination against Britain's 6.5 million disabled people. It makes all UK employers of 20 or more employees and all UK providers of goods and services legally liable for discrimination against disabled persons.

It imposes a new duty on employers and providers to make reasonable adjustments to their policies and physical environment to remove the barriers confronting disabled people. It also contains extensive provisions regulating the accessibility of public transport services — taxis, trains and buses.

The likely impact of the Act is extremely controversial. Described by the Minister for Disabled People as a 'fundamental advance ... the foundation upon which we can build to achieve the end of discrimination', it has been denounced by many disabled people as a 'bigot's charter'. The truth, as ever, lies somewhere in between, in the detail of this complex statute. It is considerably weaker than either the Sex Discrimination Act 1975 or the Race Relations Act 1976. Nevertheless, it does place disabled people on the equal opportunities agenda for the first time, and will have major ramifications for a wide range of public and private sector service providers and employers.

The 1995 Act will be brought into force in stages. Part II, relating to employment, will come into force at the end of 1996. The basic right of non-discrimination under Part III of the Act, relating to goods and services, will be introduced at the same time. The aspects of the Act requiring providers of goods and services to make reasonable adjustments to their policies and practices, to provide auxiliary aids and remove structural barriers will be introduced at a later date, to be announced by the Government after a period of consultation.

The Disability Discrimination Act 1995 applies to the whole of the United Kingdom. The principles of the Act are identical in Scotland, England, Wales and Northern Ireland. The Act does not apply where the employment, or provision of services, in question is outside the Untied Kingdom.

The author would like to thank Anne Kane for her love and support.

Caroline Gooding
December 1995

List of Abbreviations

ACAS	Advisory, Conciliation and Arbitration Service
ADA 1990	Americans with Disabilities Act 1990
BCODP	British Council of Organisations of Disabled People
CEPDs	Committees on the Employment of People with Disabilities
CRE	Commission for Racial Equality
DDA 1995	Disability Discrimination Act 1995
DEAs	Disability Employment Advisers
DP(E)A 1944	Disabled Persons (Employment) Act 1944
DPTAC	Disabled Persons Transport Advisory Committee
EOC	Equal Opportunities Commission
NACEPD	National Advisory Council on the Employment of People with Disabilities
NDC	National Disability Council
PACTs	Placement Assessment and Counselling Teams
PSV	Public service vehicle
RRA 1976	Race Relations Act 1976
SDA 1975	Sex Discrimination Act 1975

1 Introduction

There are 6.5 million disabled people in Great Britain (J. Martin, H. Meltzer and D. Elliott, *The Prevalence of Disability amongst Adults*, London: Office of Population Censuses and Surveys, 1988). Prior to the Disability Discrimination Act 1995 it was completely lawful to discriminate on the basis of disability. This new Act, key provisions of which will come into force in November 1996, will thus empower a significant proportion of the population for the first time legally to claim their right to equal participation. As the Act's requirements for the removal of the institutional and environmental barriers which confront disabled people progressively come into force, the Disability Discrimination Act may (if adequately enforced) play a significant role in opening up society to the talents of this disenfranchised minority.

Given that it represents a historic step towards the recognition of disabled people's rights, why has the Disability Discrimination Act 1995 received such a muted response, rising in some quarters to outright hostility, from disabled people themselves? Many within the Disability Movement have denounced it as a sham, a 'bigot's charter', without any teeth or real understanding of the operation of disability discrimination.

The Disability Discrimination Act 1995 is indeed a confusing, contorted and unsatisfactory piece of legislation. It signally fails to establish the clear principle of equal treatment which should be the essence of a law countering discrimination. (It has, for example, three separate definitions of what constitutes discrimination applying in different sections). The Act's fatal equivocation towards the principle of equality for disabled people has produce an extremely complicated and unclear law, hedged around with exceptions and justifications. Lord Lester, the prominent civil liberties lawyer, described it as 'riddled with vague, slippery and elusive exceptions making it so full of holes that it is more like a colander than a binding code' (Hansard, 22 May 1995, 813).

The Act's exclusion of crucial areas of social life, such as education and small businesses, makes no logical sense, and can be understood only as the product of inter-Cabinet compromises, and a concern to control potential Treasury costs.

Above all, the Act's lack of any effective enforcement mechanism undermines any claim to be a sincere attempt at ending a social evil. This crucial weakness, combined with the vagueness of certain key concepts and the absence of a timetable for the full implementation of the Act's provisions, makes it impossible to predict the actual impact of this potentially far-reaching new law.

Background

The Disability Discrimination Act (hereafter the DDA) thus bears all the hallmarks of a hasty and unwieldy political compromise. More than with most pieces of legislation, to understand the meaning of the DDA it is helpful to know its background. Why did a Conservative Government, publicly committed to deregulating business, introduce a law with precisely the rights-based approach to a social problem which is anathema to so many on the Right? The truth is that the Conservative Government produced the DDA purely as a response to political pressure, with the goal of heading off a more radical challenge in the shape of a Private Member's Bill.

The Civil Rights (Disabled Persons) Bill 1994, introduced by Harry Barnes MP, was the seventeenth attempt to introduce anti-discrimination legislation for disabled people. The first such Bill was introduced in 1982 by Jack Ashley MP (now Lord Ashley), following the recommendation of the Committee on Restrictions against Disabled People (established in 1979 by the Labour Minister for the Disabled, Alf Morris MP). A succession of back-bench Bills followed in the next ten years, with cross-party support mobilised through the All-Party Disablement Group. But it was the growth of a strong extra-Parliamentary campaign which produced the final breakthrough, pushing the issue high up the political agenda where it could no longer be ignored by the Government.

The vehicle for the campaign was Voluntary Organisations for Anti-Discrimination Legislation, formed in 1985 and subsequently renamed as the Right Now Campaign. This campaign united a broad range of traditional charities such as the Royal Association for Disability and Rehabilitation with younger, more militant organisations of disabled people, most notably the British Council of Organisations of Disabled People (BCODP). Such organisations were themselves the product of the radicalisation of disabled people, angered by the continuing discrimination and poverty confronting them in their daily lives. Towards the end of the 1980s this Disability Movement began to adopt strategies such as sit-ins and street demonstrations to highlight its demands, the most prominent of which was for civil rights.

The British campaign was encouraged in its demands, and helped to formulate them with increasing confidence and sophistication, by the example of disabled people in America. The Americans with Disabilities Act (ADA) 1990 represents the most comprehensive and far-reaching attempt to legislate for equal rights for disabled people. It grew from the experience of implementing an earlier, more limited anti-discrimination measure (the Rehabilitation Act 1973), and from extensive political lobbying and grass-roots activism.

The American example helped inspire and provide a model for similar legislation in Canada, Australia and New Zealand. Many of the key concepts of the ADA 1990 were incorporated into the Civil Rights (Disabled Persons) Bill, introduced by Alf Morris MP (now a back-bencher) in 1991 and 1992, and by Roger Berry MP in 1993.

The Government was able to defeat these Bills by procedural mechanisms. But by 1994 the political momentum behind the campaign, with support from back-bench Conservatives threatening to overturn the Government's increasingly fragile majority, was such that the Government announced that it would bring forward its own proposals to counter disability discrimination and published a Consultative Document (*A Consultation on Government Measures to Tackle Discrimination against Disabled People*, Department of Social Security, 1994).

The Disability Discrimination Bill was introduced barely six months after the publication of this Consultative Document. Its Parliamentary progress was hastened to ensure that it took precedence over the Civil Rights Bill, reintroduced by Harry Barnes MP.

The DDA's extensive exclusions, inadequate enforcement mechanisms, tentative draftsmanship and concern for tight Government control over its subsequent interpretation through the courts, is the product of this last minute, half-hearted conversion. The haste with which the Act has been produced creates an unfinished air, with many crucial issues still unresolved. The cost ceiling and timetable for the adjustments which will be required of providers of goods and services will, for example, be critical in determining the impact of the Act, and will not be announced until 1996.

Before plunging into the detail of the Act it will be helpful to explore in more detail the nature of discrimination faced by disabled people, and the sort of legal concepts which have been developed to counter it.

Disability Discrimination

Discrimination is not a term which historically has been associated with disabled people. Despite an increasing recognition of the importance of institutional discrimination in perpetuating the disadvantaged positions of women and black people, discrimination is still understood by most people to mean the treatment of a person less favourably because of hostility, or stereotypes. This form of discrimination certainly exists against disabled people.

A recent report by Liberty (*Access Denied, human rights and disabled people*, London, Liberty, 1994) cited the following examples of discrimination:

— a holiday camp refused a booking from a group with cerebral palsy
— a property owner refused to sell or allow occupation of land by people with a history of mental health problems
— a landlord banned a disabled skittles team from a public house because he believed some of its members to be 'mentally handicapped'
— an oil company refused to employ people who are HIV positive
— a blind doctor was prevented from taking her guide dog into Buckingham Palace where she had been invited to receive an award from the Queen
— an employer refused to hire a qualified blind telesales person because its office was on the first floor and the employer thought that blind people could not walk up stairs.

But more powerful than individual prejudices are the unintended, institutional forms of discrimination. Anne Begg, a disabled teacher, writes vividly about the impact of these on her everyday life (*Civil Rights for Disabled People*, London: TUC, 1995):

Imagine a world where there was a barrier across the doors of most shops on the high street which read 'Sorry, no women beyond this point'.

Or a world where every time you go out, be it to a pub, restaurant, shopping or wherever, you then find that there are no toilets for you, or that the ones they have constructed for you are full of furniture.

Or a world where the only way you can travel on some British Rail trains is in the guards van, while you're not allowed on most buses or in the London Underground at all simply because you happen to be black. . . .

Or where a cinema which has just allowed a drunk man to enter with a fag hanging out of his mouth, turns round and says 'You can't come in here because you've got bright red hair and you're a fire hazard' . . .

If such social apartheid occurred to you just because you were male or female or black, there would, quite rightly, be a public outcry. The gross unfairness of such treatment is so clear. Yet all of the above, and much more, has happened to me at some time in my life.

And my crime? I use a wheelchair to get around.

Procedures and practices which do not take into account disabled people (like the 'no dogs' rule at Buckingham Palace), buildings and vehicles which are built without a thought for disabled users, are not intended to discriminate, but they have this effect just the same. And the cumulative result of a society which has been designed to exclude and segregate disabled people into their own, 'special' provision is devastating:

— The average income of disabled people under retirement age is just 72 per cent of the average income of all people within this age group
— Disabled adults are two and half times as likely to be unemployed as non-disabled adults
— Profoundly deaf children, who are no less intelligent than other children, nevertheless have an average reading age of 8 when they leave school because of their second-class education
— There are 4 million people with mobility impairments, but only 80,000 accessible homes
— A survey of disabled people found that four out of five of the people interviewed had problems with transport, and two-thirds said that difficulty using public transport was one reason for not going out more and not travelling further afield.

(Statistics are from *Civil Rights for Disabled People*, London: TUC, 1995. A comprehensive account is available in C. Barnes, *Disabled People in Britain*, London: Hurst & Co., 1991.)

When this poverty and unequal participation in society is recognised, it historically has been explained as the consequence of disabled people's own inherent physical or mental functional limitations (their impairments), to be addressed through charity and separate provision. This approach is known as the 'medical model', in contrast to the 'social model' which emphasises instead the role of social institutions and attitudes in disabling people with impairments. An acceptance of the social model (albeit half-hearted in the case of the DDA) and a recognition of the role that unfair treatment plays in excluding disabled people, forms the essential underpinning for any law countering disability discrimination.

Legislating against Disability Discrimination

The laws against sex and race discrimination seek to address not only direct discrimination (hostile attitudes or stereotypes), but also institutional discrimination.

The latter is addressed through the concept of indirect discrimination in the Sex Discrimination Act (SDA) 1975 and the Race Relations Act (RRA) 1976. Where an apparently neutral condition or requirement has an adverse impact on members of a particular ethnic group or gender, and this discriminatory effect cannot be justified by the reasonable needs of the organisation, it will constitute unlawful, indirect discrimination.

Thus, for example, in the USA a requirement that all applicants for manual labourers' jobs should have a high school diploma was held in one case to be discriminatory because, in the southern states of America in the 1970s, considerably fewer black people were able to meet this requirement, and because such a qualification could not be shown to be relevant to the jobs in question.

The American disability legislation uses the concepts of direct and indirect discrimination, but added a third one which emphasised the need to dismantle the environmental barriers faced by disabled people. The concept of 'reasonable accommodation' originated in cases of religious discrimination where organisations might be obliged to provide a reasonable accommodation to the requirements of a particular religion, for example, by allowing flexible shifts for those not permitted to work on Saturdays. The regulations promulgated under the US Rehabilitation Act 1973, and subsequently the ADA 1990, required employers and service providers to provide reasonable accommodations to the need of disabled employees.

As with the law concerning indirect discrimination, this concept attempts to balance the rights of disabled people to a barrier-free environment against the ability of organisations to sustain the cost of providing such an environment. The ADA 1990 used the additional concepts of programme accessibility and undue hardship, as well as detailed regulations, to indicate how this balance should be struck in interpreting what accommodations would be reasonable.

The Disability Discrimination Act 1995

The conceptual framework of the DDA 1995 differs from both the British sex and race legislation and the American disability legislation. This means that caution must be exercised in using precedents from these other laws. (Although this book will, where relevant, indicate where the DDA does follow the model of previous Acts.)

The first difference is that under the DDA direct discrimination (i.e., treating an individual less favourably on the basis of the disability) can be legally 'justified'. This is not the case with any other anti-discrimination laws.

The Government justifies this distinction on the basis that, unlike with race or gender, disability may be relevant to a person's ability to perform a job. However, it is not true that race or gender can never be relevant to such a decision. The SDA 1975, for example, exempts any employment in which being a man (or woman) is a genuine occupational qualification of the job, as defined in some detail by the legislation. The American legislation (and the British Civil Rights Bill) takes a similar approach by restricting rights to 'qualified' disabled people, defined as those who are able to perform the 'essential functions' of the job.

The DDA's approach is to incorporate 'justifications' into the definition of discrimination, so that discrimination is defined as less favourable treatment for a reason related to a person's disability *which cannot be justified under the Act*. Because the justifications differ within the different sections of the Act this produces different definitions of discrimination for employment, goods and services and premises. Not only is this approach confusing, but also many of justifications are themselves dangerously vague.

The second difference from other anti-discrimination laws is that the DDA 1995 does not include the concept of indirect discrimination (perhaps because of its successful use in a string of sex discrimination cases against the Government in recent years). It may be that the basic definition of disability discrimination is sufficient to catch some elements of indirect discrimination, because it is somewhat broader than the comparable term for direct discrimination in the SDA 1975 or RRA 1976. Less favourable treatment 'for a reason which relates to the disabled person's disability' may, depending on its interpretation through case law, turn out to be quite a broad concept. For example, if a person is excluded from opening an account because he or she cannot produce a driving licence, and the reason why that person does not have a licence is connected to his or her disability, then this could be said to be for 'a reason related to' that disability.

The DDA does, in addition to this basic definition of discrimination, incorporate the American concept of reasonable accommodation (albeit in a more restrictive form). Except in relation to premises, discrimination is also defined as a failure to comply with a duty to provide 'reasonable adjustment'. Once again the definition of what constitutes a 'reasonable adjustment' varies between each section of the Act. The Government clearly intends that unintentionally discriminatory barriers will be addressed by this means, to this extent reducing the need for the concept of indirect discrimination.

The other significant difference from other discrimination laws lies not so much in the conceptual framework as in the enforcement mechanisms. The essence of such laws is that they confer a right on individuals not to suffer discrimination. This structure is a strength in the sense that it does not rely on a possibly unenthusiastic and overburdened state machinery for action. However, it has also been criticised for relying too heavily on isolated, possibly ill-informed and under-resourced individuals. The British sex and race discrimination laws recognised this problem by creating the Equal Opportunities Commission and Commission for Racial Equality and investing them with a broad range of pro-active investigatory powers. The American ADA 1990 is similarly enforced by a range of Government agencies such as the Equal Employment Opportunities Commission. The DDA 1995, by failing to establish a strategic enforcement agency, effectively ignores this problem. Instead of a commission, it establishes an advisory body, the National Disability Council, described by Lord Lester as a 'pathetically powerless quango' (Hansard, 22 May 1995, 815). In addition, a network of assistance agencies has been promised, with regard to the right of access to goods and services, the details of which have yet to be revealed.

The DDA also differs from other discrimination laws by excluding large sections of social life from its coverage: the police, prison and armed services and firms with fewer than 20 employees are excluded from Part II, while education is excluded from Part III. Transport is addressed in a curiously hybrid fashion: in so far as the issue concerns the transport infrastructure, the right of access to goods and services applies; in so far as the problem relates to vehicles, it is addressed through regulations establishing construction standards enforced by various statutory agencies.

Lord Lester castigated the DDA's retreat from the established principles of equality legislation: 'Another basic and universally recognised concept in discrimination law is that all exceptions to the principles of equal treatment should be kept to the minimum necessary to avoid undermining the principle itself.' In existing laws exceptions are usually carefully and narrowly defined. 'By contrast this Bill embodies a series of sweepingly broad absolute exceptions.' (Hansard, 22 May 1995, 813)

Future Developments

The Government has indicated that Part II of the DDA, relating to employment, will come into force at the end of 1996. The White Paper indicated that the Government would consult over the timetable for the implementation of Part III of the Act, relating to goods and services, suggesting that it might start by prohibiting discriminatory conditions of access, policies, procedures and practices, followed by the provision of auxiliary aids and then the removal of structural barriers (*Ending Discrimination against Disabled People*, London: HMSO, 1995, p. 27). This consultation is likely to take place early in 1996. It is clear that at least some of the Part III rights will come into force at the end of 1996.

The timetable of the accessibility requirements for public transport contained in Part V of the Act has not been indicated.

Many of the 1995 Act's key terms lack precision. It is to be hoped that the Codes of Practice, which the Secretary of State has the power to issue with regard to both employment and the provision of goods and services, and the guidance on aspects of the definition of disability, will clarify the scope and meaning of the Act. Draft Codes and guidance are likely to be issued early in 1996.

The DDA also contains extensive regulation-making powers. It is unclear to what extent currently it is planned to use these. The Government has, however, indicated that it intends to consult on draft proposals for regulations in Part III on:

(a)   the type of auxiliary aids to be provided, and circumstances in which they would be required;

(b)   the structural barriers which would have to be removed and when this would be appropriate;

(c)   the alternatives to removing barriers;

(d)   the need for financial barriers on the cost of providing such adjustments;

(e)   possible exemptions to the new right (*Ending Discrimination against Disabled People,* London: HMSO, 1995, p. 26).

It is also likely to be consulting on regulations spelling out the requirement for the insurance industry.

It is clear that over the next year, this secondary legislation may significantly clarify, restrict or expand the scope of the DDA 1995. Political pressure over subsequent years may lead to other significant alterations. For example, the exemption of small employers must be reviewed within five years of the passage of the Act, and this may lead to its reduction or abolition.

As these developments unfold, and case law accumulates, it will become much clearer whether the DDA is capable of combating disability discrimination, or whether its compromised terms and lack of effective implementation mechanisms mean that it will fail to have a substantial impact.

Meanwhile the Rights Now Campaign has indicated that it will not rest until its goal of full, effective and enforceable civil rights for disabled people has been achieved, and may secure substantial revisions to bring the Act more in line with the Civil Rights Bill 1994.

2 Who is Protected? The Definition of Disability

While previous equality laws prohibit discrimination against anyone whenever it is based on specific grounds (gender, race or religion), the DDA 1995 protects against less favourable treatment on the basis of disability only if a person is disabled. This means that non-disabled people are not able legally to challenge preferential treatment given to disabled people in the way that white people and men have been able to use the RRA 1976 and SDA 1975. It also means that in order to bring proceedings under the DDA 1995, a person must first establish that he or she falls within the Act's definition of a disabled person.

Overview

The DDA 1995 creates a new legal definition of 'disabled person'. It does not, however, replace the previous definitions of disability or 'handicap' contained in other legislation (with one exception discussed below). Neither is there any direct connection with these other legal definitions. The fact that an individual has, for example, been able to qualify for the disabled living allowance or incapacity benefit does not automatically mean that he or she will come within the DDA's definition — although clearly there will be a considerable overlap.

However, because the DDA repeals large sections of the Disabled Persons (Employment) Act (DP(E)A) 1944, including the sections establishing a register for 'occupationally handicapped' persons, it does substitute its definition of 'disabled person' for the one contained in that Act (DDA 1995, s. 61(5)), and also provides that persons registered under the 1944 Act will be deemed to be disabled under the terms of the DDA for a period of three years from the employment provisions of the 1995 Act coming into force (DDA 1995, sch. 1, para. 7(1)). (Such persons must have been on the register on 12 January 1995, and on the date when the employment provisions take effect.)

Although the 1995 Act establishes a new definition of 'disabled person', it does not reflect any fundamentally new understanding of disability. The Act's definition of disability was, precisely for this reason, one of the most contentious issues during its passage through Parliament. Like the definitions contained in previous legislation, it focuses solely on the inability to perform certain physical or mental functions caused directly by the 'impairments' of an individual.

The disability lobby, and their supporters in Parliament, criticised this as overly restrictive and stemming from a flawed conceptualisation of disability. They argued for a broader definition of disability, modelled on that contained in the American

ADA 1990. The key distinction was that the preferred definition would have included people who were perceived to be disabled. Such an approach would have focused on the issue of social discrimination — which precisely stems from the misconceptions and stereotypes of the discriminator rather than from any intrinsic characteristic of the individual who has experienced discrimination.

The DDA's basic definition cannot address the situation of people with no actual physical or mental limitations, who nevertheless experience strong social restrictions because of prejudice. Thus, people with severe disfigurement, a highly stigmatised group, do not fall within the Act's core definition, and have to be brought in as an exceptional group. Where a person has a severe disfigurement, this will be deemed to have a substantial adverse effect on his or her ability to carry out normal day-to-day activities, thus bringing him or her within the definition of the Act (DDA 1995, sch. 1, para. 3).

Other highly stigmatised groups of people are excluded from the Act's definition of 'disability' altogether. Thus, people who have been diagnosed as being HIV positive will not initially be protected from discrimination. It is only once they begin to develop symptoms that bring them within the special clause regarding people with progressive conditions (see below) that they will be entitled to protection under the Act. And yet, prejudice and stereotypes begin from the moment of diagnosis, not from the development of an impairment.

The Government amended the Bill to extend coverage to persons with a history of a disability, a move that was regarded as a considerable concession to the disability lobby, because it moves away from an emphasis on actual bodily restrictions to a recognition of the power of social stigma.

Far from achieving the Government's stated goal of mirroring a 'common-sense' understanding of disability, the Act's definition is actually very complex and counter-intuitive. The attempt to provide a tightly drawn and controlled definition of the beneficiaries of the new law (perhaps influenced by its origin within the Department of Social Security) produces a Kafkaesque result, which twists and strains logic.

As elsewhere, the Secretary of State has extensive powers to expand upon, or alter, the basic provisions of the Act. He has the power to issue guidance regarding different aspects of the definition (s. 3); specify 'conditions' which will or will not be taken to amount to an impairment (sch. 1, para. 1(2)); deem that an impairment which is not long-term is, and vice versa (sch. 1, para. 2(4)), and that an impairment which does not affect one of the prescribed list of activities will be taken to do so, or vice versa (sch. 1, para. 4(2)).

Core Definition

To be protected against discrimination under the 1995 Act an individual must either be a disabled person (defined as 'a person who has a disability' (s. 1(2)), or be a person who has had such a disability (s. 2).

A disability is defined as either a physical or a mental impairment, which has a substantial and long-term adverse effect on a person's ability to carry out normal day-to-day activities (s. 1(1)).

Note that the substantial long-term effect must stem from an impairment. If a person has a number of absences from work due to sickness, which stem from a number of different, short-term ailments, this will not constitute an impairment. If, however, a person develops AIDS, and as a result has a number of periods of sickness, these will constitute an impairment provided that the reason for developing them was the reduced effectiveness of the immune system resulting from the HIV virus.

The definition thus logically breaks down into four components, which must be satisfied if a person is to be protected by the 1995 Act:

(a) there must be a 'physical or mental impairment'; and

(b) the impairment must adversely affect the individual's 'ability to carry out normal day-to-day activities'; and

(c) the adverse effect must be 'substantial'; and

(d) the adverse effect must be 'long-term'.

What is an impairment?

The Minister, in the course of explaining that this phrase covered people with sensory impairments, indicated that 'The terms physical and mental are intended to be seen in their widest sense and should comprehensively cover all forms of impairment' (Hague, Hansard, 2 February 1995, 71).

No elaboration of the term 'physical impairment' is provided in the DDA 1995. However, sch. 1, para. 1(1) further qualifies the term 'mental impairment'. A person with a mental illness will be regarded as having a mental impairment for the purposes of the Act only if the mental illness is 'clinically well-recognised'. This phrase is a novel one, appearing in no previous mental health legislation. The Minister explained that it was intended to refer to a situation in which 'a substantial body of practitioners . . . accept that such a condition exists', and to exclude 'moods or mild eccentricities' (Hague, Hansard, 7 February 1995, 104).

Schedule 1, para. 1(2) gives the Secretary of State the power to exclude or include certain conditions from coverage by the term 'impairment'. The Minister indicated that he intended to use this power to exclude 'psychopathic or antisocial disorders and addictions', such as 'kleptomania, pyromania, paedophilia and personality disorders' (Hague, Hansard, 7 February 1995, 105). It will be interesting to see whether this power is also used to exclude drug and alcohol addictions, both of which are included within the American legislation.

What are normal day-to-day activities?

An impairment's adverse effect will be relevant only if it restricts the ability to carry out one of a prescribed and finite list of 'normal day-to-day activities' contained in sch. 1, para. 4: mobility; manual dexterity; physical co-ordination; continence; ability to lift, carry or otherwise move everyday objects; speech, hearing or eyesight; memory or ability to learn or understand; the ability to concentrate; and the perception of risk of physical danger.

This list is exhaustive, rather than merely illustrative. However, it is clear that the categories are intended to be fairly broad.

For example, in Parliamentary debates it was indicated that 'the ability to stand, to sit, to rise from sitting, to breathe, to move confidently outside the home and to cope with unfamiliar environments . . . are all essential to normal mobility (Lord Mackay,

Hansard, 13 June 1995, 1672). Similarly it was indicated that the category 'speech, hearing or eyesight' was intended to capture the broader aspects of ability to communicate with other people, which did not otherwise fall within the phrase 'memory or ability to concentrate, learn or understand'.

The ability to remain conscious (relevant, for example, to people with narcolepsy or epilepsy) would be regarded as an essential prerequisite for carrying out any of the categories of activity.

The ability to breathe would likewise be important for several categories of activity — mobility, ability to lift and speech.

The breadth of these categories ensures that many more physical or mental conditions come within the definition than would at first sight be apparent. However, when the qualifying term 'substantial' (in s. 1(1)) is introduced, the way in which the categories are constructed may introduce additional exclusions. For example, someone might have substantial breathing difficulties which have an impact on his or her mobility, but not a substantial impact. They would therefore fall outside the definition.

The impact of an impairment is measured with regard to its effect on 'normal day-to-day activities'. The issue which has been stressed in this regard is that the question is whether or not the activity in question is a normal activity for the population as a whole, rather than for the specific person.

> [W]e say 'normal day-to-day activities' to avoid people thinking that it covers ability to participate in some specialised sport or activity that most of us would not be capable of anyway and would not regard as part of normal day-to-day life. (Hague, Hansard, 7 February 1995, 120).

This is likely to have particular relevance where the activity which is affected is one that is required by a person's work. The inability to perform a specialised work activity will not in itself qualify an individual to be counted as disabled under the Act, unless the impairment also has an impact on some more generalised activity.

Effects of pain, stress and fatigue   The scope of the definition is further extended because if an impairment causes stress, fatigue or pain these effects will be taken into account in determining whether or not it produces a substantial effect on a person's ability to perform day-to-day activities.

What is meant by substantial?

Whether or not an effect is 'substantial' is likely to be a crucial, and contested, point. The Minister's explanation was that the effect of the impairment should be 'more than minor', and was intended to exclude 'trivial matters' from the scope of the legislation (Hansard, 7 February 1995, 82).

What is meant by long-term effect?

Schedule 1, para. 2 elaborates on what is meant by this phrase. The effect must have lasted at least 12 months, or be expected to last either 12 months or for the rest of the individual's life (in the case of terminally ill people, with a shorter life expectancy).

Extending the Core Definition

Fluctuating conditions People with fluctuating and recurring conditions, an individual episode of which might not last 12 months, are brought within the definition by sch. 1, para. 2(2), which provides:

Where an impairment ceases to have a substantial adverse effect on a person's ability to carry out normal day-to-day activities, it is to be treated as continuing to have that effect if that effect is likely to recur.

Questions that may arise under this provision are how long the original, substantially adverse effect has to last in the first place, and how likely it needs to be to recur. It is clear, for example, that persons with epilepsy are intended to be covered. The effect of an epileptic seizure may last only a few minutes, and may have only a slight chance of recurring; nevertheless, the label of epilepsy can have a substantial effect on an individual's job prospects.

Medication The effects of control by medication or special aids should be ignored in assessing whether or not an impairment has a continuing and substantial adverse effect (sch. 1, para. 6). The examples given in the course of debates were the control of epilepsy by medication, and the use of prosthetic limbs. However, people whose sight impairment can be corrected by the wearing of spectacles and contact lenses are covered only if a substantial adverse effect remains despite those appliances (sch. 1, para. 6(2)).

There are two classes of impairment singled out for separate treatment.

Severe disfigurement People with severe disfigurements are deemed to satisfy the condition regarding a 'substantial adverse effect' on day-to-day activities (sch. 1, para. 3). Provided that the disfigurement is a long-term one, or one which is likely to recur (for example, eczema), such individuals will be regarded as disabled for the purposes of the 1995 Act.

Progressive conditions Where a person has a progressive condition and, as a result of this condition, has (or had) an impairment which has (or had) an adverse effect on his or her ability to carry out a normal day-to-day activity, this effect will, by virtue of sch. 1, para. 8(1), be deemed to be substantial, provided that the condition is likely to lead to such an impairment.

This means that if an individual with a progressive condition begins to experience symptoms which have an effect, however slight, on one of the prescribed list of categories of activity, he or she will be taken to fall within the Act's definition of a disabled person. This will remain the case even if those symptoms disappear (for example, people with multiple sclerosis may experience periods of remission).

However, not all persons with progressive conditions will be protected by the DDA 1995 from the point of diagnosis; only those people who have (or have had, in the case of people experiencing a remission) symptoms affecting the prescribed list of categories of activity in some way (or who would have such symptoms if they were not taking medication) will be so protected.

The term 'progressive condition' is not defined, although some examples are included on the face of the Act (cancer, HIV, multiple sclerosis and muscular dystrophy), and regulations may provide further clarification.

Guidance

The Secretary of State has the power to issue guidance about the matters to be taken into account in determining whether an impairment has a substantial long-term effect on a person's ability to carry out normal day-to-day activities (s. 3). Such guidance is likely to include examples of effects on activities which would, and would not, count as 'substantial' and 'long-term'.

The status of such guidance is similar to that of the Codes of Practice for employment and services. When determining whether or not the impact of an individual's impairment is sufficient to bring him or her within the Act's definition of a disabled person, a tribunal must take into account any aspect of the guidance which appears relevant (s. 3(3)).

3 Employment

The overwhelming majority of cases brought under the sex and race discrimination legislation have been employment cases. While there may, for a number of reasons, be a greater emphasis on access to goods and services under the DDA 1995, the success or failure of the employment provisions, which will be brought into force first, will inevitably be scrutinised closely.

A glance at the operation of the American ADA 1990 provides an indication as to the sort of cases which might be expected under the DDA 1995. Approximately half of the complaints filed under the employment provisions of the ADA 1990 in its first 18 months alleged discriminatory discharge. This follows a similar pattern in race and sex discrimination claims in both Britain and America, partly because the stake of losing a current job is greater than that of failing to obtain a new job, and partly because the issues tend to be clearer and easier to prove. A further 13 per cent of complaints concerned hiring, 10 per cent concerned alleged harassment, and 4 per cent concerned employee benefits. Twenty three per cent of the ADA employment complaints alleged a failure to provide a reasonable accommodation, an indication of the central importance of this concept. (See J. Coil and C. Rice, 'The Tip of the Iceberg: Early Trends in ADA Enforcement', *Employee Relations Law Journal*, Spring 1994, vol. 19.)

The types of disability associated with the American ADA claims are also instructive. Back impairments were the largest category, accounting for 20 per cent of claims (often relating to dismissal after extended periods of sick leave). People with 'mental impairments' (mental health problems or brain injuries) amounted to 10 per cent of claimants.

What is Discrimination in Employment?

Discrimination is defined in two ways in Part II of the DDA 1995:

(a)   Less favourable treatment. An employer discriminates against a disabled person if, for a reason which relates to a person's disability, he treats the disabled person less favourably than he would treat a person to whom the reason does not apply *and* he cannot show that the treatment is justified (s. 5(1)).

(b)   Reasonable adjustment. An employer discriminates against a disabled person if he fails to provide such reasonable adjustments to the working environment as are required by s. 6 of the Act, *and* he cannot justify this failure (s. 5(2)).

Positive discrimination

Because discrimination is defined by the DDA 1995 in an asymmetrical way, as only applying to a disabled person, this means that less favourable treatment of a non-disabled person is lawful, even when the decision is made on the basis of disability. That is to say that positive discrimination in favour of a disabled person is not restricted by the DDA 1995. This is a very important distinction from the position with regard to positive discrimination on the basis of race or sex, where the RRA 1976 and SDA 1975 tightly restrict the situations in which such behaviour is lawful.

Consequently, employers can lawfully advertise that certain posts are only available to disabled applicants. However, as far as local authorities are concerned their ability to positively discriminate in this way is removed by the Local Government and Housing Act 1989. Section 7(1) of that Act requires 'every appointment to a paid office or employment under a local authority or parish or community council in England and Wales, or a local authority in Scotland' to be 'made on merit'.

Previously the effect of this section on positive discrimination for disabled people was removed because s. 7(2) made it subject to the provisions of the Disabled Persons (Employment) Act 1944 regarding the operation of the quota scheme. The relevant provisions of this Act will be repealed when the employment provisions of the DDA 1995 come into force (see below), and DDA 1995, sch. 6, para. 5 inserts into the Local Government and Housing Act 1989 instead a new s. 7(2)(f), making this 'merit principle' subject only to local authorities' duties to provide reasonable adjustments, and not to treat disabled people less favourably without justification. The effect is to prohibit certain forms of discrimination in favour of disabled people in employment by local authorities.

The only other restriction concerning positive discrimination is that it will generally be unlawful to give preferential treatment to one disabled person over another disabled person, if it is on the grounds of their disability. However, where the goal of a charity requires it to confer benefits on a particular group of persons 'determined by reference to any physical or mental capacity', actions taken in pursuance of such a goal will not be unlawful (DDA 1995, s. 10). This would, for example, allow an organisation established for the benefit of blind people to employ a blind person rather than a deaf person, specifically for reasons related to disability.

Less favourable treatment

This concept differs in a number of ways from the prohibitions against direct discrimination in the SDA 1975 and RRA 1976, most notably because the DDA 1995 allows direct discrimination to be justified. This clearly represents a significant weakening of the core concept of discrimination.

Nevertheless, an employer's ability to justify his actions is substantially constrained by the requirement that any such justification take into account the duty to make reasonable adjustments. Thus, for example, if an employer sought to justify rejecting an applicant for a post on the basis that that applicant could not answer the telephone, the employer would need to show that no reasonable adjustment (e.g., installing a minicom or transferring telephone duties to another member of staff) would resolve this problem.

It is a clearly established principle under existing discrimination laws that the motivation for an act of direct discrimination is irrelevant (*R* v *Birmingham City Council ex parte Equal Opportunities Commission* [1989] IRLR 173, HL). The issue is solely whether or not sex or race or religion constituted a factor in the decision. Provided that it did influence the decision, it is irrelevant whether an employer acted from a 'benign' motive, which he or she felt was in the best interest of the employee. Under the DDA 1995, because less favourable treatment on the grounds of disability may be justified, the reason for the action becomes very relevant.

This is likely to lead to a very different pattern of cases under the 1995 Act. Whereas cases of sex or race discrimination almost invariably involve employers denying that sex or race played a role, employers in many DDA cases will admit that disability influenced their decision. The crucial issues will then be whether or not the decision can be justified, and whether or not a reasonable adjustment would be feasible.

Some principles established through sex and race litigation will still be relevant. For example, it should not be necessary to show that disability was the sole ground for a decision, provided it substantially influenced the decision (*Owen & Briggs* v *James* [1982] IRLR 502, CA). Indeed, an individual may also have been discriminated against on grounds of race or sex, and may bring forward several claims at the same time.

Justifications for discrimination   Once a complainant has shown that the reason for less favourable treatment relates to his or her disability, it is for the employer to show that the treatment in question was justified. To justify less favourable treatment an employer must show that the reason for the treatment was both material to the circumstances of the particular case and substantial (s. 5(3)). 'Material' has been interpreted as meaning 'significant and relevant' to the particular circumstances (*Rainey* v *Greater Glasgow Health Board* [1987] IRLR 26, HL).

The Minister indicated during debates that 'substantial' meant 'more than minor', and was intended to exclude 'trivial matters' from the scope of the legislation (Hansard, 7 February 1995, 82). However the House of Lords interpreted the word in the following way:

Substantial ... is not the same as 'not insubstantial' ... One of the primary meanings of the word is equivalent to considerable, solid or big. It is in this sense that we speak of a substantial fortune, a substantial meal, a substantial man, a substantial argument or ground of defence. (*Palser* v *Grinling* [1948] AC 291, HL.)

What makes this test much harder for an employer to fulfil is that the employer's decision must have taken into account his or her duty to make reasonable adjustments (see below). Thus, if the material reason for less favourable treatment could have been resolved by a reasonable adjustment, then the decision cannot be justified. (This will only apply, however, where the less favourable treatment puts the disabled person at a 'substantial' disadvantage, as this is the precondition for the reasonable adjustment duty to come into effect.) The law will not require employers to engage in actions which are clearly futile. Section 5(5) provides that if an employer can show that his or her treatment would have been justified even after providing a reasonable adjustment, then in these circumstances the employer will not be guilty of unlawful discrimination if he or she fails to provide such a reasonable adjustment.

Parliamentary debates shed little light on the intended scope of these justifications, and it is likely that the courts will place particular reliance on the code of practice in this area. It is nevertheless possible to suggest several general principles.

Stereotypes   An employer cannot act upon generalised fears. For example, a job applicant with a history of mental illness could not be refused employment on the general ground that the job would be stressful, and that this might trigger a recurrence of the problem. However, an individualised assessment of the risk, carried out by an expert, taking into account the feasibility of reasonable adjustments, might justify rejecting an applicant on this ground.

Blanket exclusion   The current practice of excluding a class of people with a specific impairment (for example, people with epilepsy or diabetes) from certain jobs would need to be justified in each individual case, and in many cases an individualised assessment of the abilities of the applicant or employee would be required. This will apply particularly where the functional effects of an impairment take a wide variety of forms, some of which could be accommodated through reasonable adjustments.

Health and safety   Health and safety issues have in the past frequently been cited as reasons for not employing disabled individuals. Where there is a conflict, other statutory provisions take precedence over the DDA 1995 (s. 59). Under the Health and Safety at Work etc. Act 1974, employers have a duty to provide safe fellow employees, and a duty to third parties not to expose them to risk. If an employer can show that, *regardless of any reasonable adjustments which he or she might make,* a disabled applicant would expose fellow employees or third parties to risk, then this would constitute a lawful justification for refusing to employ that applicant.

Nevertheless, it is essential that an individual assessment is made, and consideration is first given to the possibility of reasonable adjustments removing the risk. A Canadian case (*Erickson* v *Canadian Pacific Express & Transport Ltd* (1987) 87 CLLC para. 17,005, Can. HRT) illustrates this point. It involved a truck driver who became hearing impaired and who began to use a hearing aid. He was dismissed because the company had a blanket policy against employing hearing-aid users. A finding of discrimination was made because the employee met federal standards and licensing requirements, and there was no evidence that the employer had examined the employee on an individual basis for increased safety risk.

The same principle would apply, for example, if an employer assumed that a wheelchair user would constitute a safety risk in evacuating a work place. Prior to rejecting such an applicant, an employer would have to consider the possibility of instituting appropriate procedures for reducing the safety risk.

Note that regulations may make provision as to the circumstances in which treatment is, or is not, deemed to be justified (s. 5(6)).

Reason related to disability?   While an employer's ability to justify less favourable treatment results in a more limited meaning being given to 'discrimination', in other ways the differences in wording of the DDA's definition of discrimination suggests that it may reach further than the comparable provision in the sex and race legislation.

Discrimination can be alleged if a decision was 'for a reason which relates to' an individual's disability, whereas under the SDA 1975 and RRA 1976 a decision must shown to be 'on the ground of' sex or race. To illustrate the difference, a person who was unable to work full-time because of his or her disability, and was dismissed from a post for this reason, could challenge that decision under the DDA 1995 because it was for a reason related to that person's disability. In contrast, a claim for direct sex or race discrimination could be made only by showing that a person of a different race or sex would have been allowed to work part-time.

The breadth of the less favourable treatment standard in the 1995 Act means that issues such as this, which might have been addressed through the indirect discrimination provisions of the SDA 1975 and RRA 1976 (which have no equivalent in the DDA), can be tackled under the DDA's basic prohibition against less favourable treatment in s. 5(1).

One issue which will need to be clarified, either through the Code of Practice to be issued by the Secretary of State, or through case law, is how tight a causal connection is implied by the term 'which relates to'. For example, if a person lacks the required academic standard for a post because of the sub-standard schooling he or she has received in a special school, would rejection on this basis count as a reason related to that person's disability?

Less favourable than whom?   A claim for direct discrimination relies on comparing the treatment of the alleged victim of discrimination with that of another person, and showing that the alleged victim has been treated less favourably because of sex or race or disability. In sex and race discrimination laws the comparison must be with persons of a different sex or racial background in the same or not materially different circumstances (SDA 1975, s. 5; RRA 1976, s. 3).

The comparison which is established by the DDA 1995 is more precise, in that it focuses on the reason for the discrimination. A disabled person who alleges discrimination for a reason related to his or her disability must compare his or her treatment with the treatment of a person to whom the reason for less favourable treatment does not apply. This might be an able bodied person, or a person with a different impairment, since what might constitute a barrier for a person with a learning disability, might not cause a problem for someone with arthritis.

The comparison might even be made with person with a similar impairment. Thus, if a blind person had been rejected for a job, it would not be enough for an employer to show that he or she had appointed another visually impaired person. Instead, the question would be: Why was the applicant rejected? If it was for a reason related to the applicant's disability (for example, if he or she relied on a guide dog and the employer did not want a dog in the offices) and this reason did not apply to the successful applicant (a blind person who did not use a guide dog) then less favourable treatment would have been established and the issue would focus on whether it could be justified.

Duty to make reasonable adjustments

Where any arrangements made by or behalf of an employer, or any physical features of premises occupied by an employer, place a disabled employee or applicant at a substantial disadvantage in comparison with persons who are not disabled, the employer must take such steps as are reasonable under all the circumstances to prevent the disadvantageous effect (DDA 1995, s. 6(1)).

When does the duty arise?   There is no general duty on employers to act pro-actively so as to make their work places more accessible to disabled employees. Instead, the duty to make reasonable adjustments is owed to individual disabled persons when the relevant circumstances arise.

The duty is not owed to disabled applicants or employees unless the employer knows, or could reasonably be expected to know, that they have a disability and as a result are placed at a substantial disadvantage by their work arrangements or premises (s. 6(6)(b)). For example, unless a deaf person informs a prospective employer in advance that a signer will be required for an interview, an employer will not be expected to make arrangements for one. However, if a wheelchair user arrives for an interview and finds that the premises are inaccessible, the employer would be obliged to consider whether it was possible (and 'reasonable') to arrange the interview in an accessible room. The duty does not arise toward potential applicants unless they have told the employer that they may apply for the job (s. 6(6)(a)).

Furthermore, the duty arises only where a disabled person is placed at a *substantial* disadvantage by arrangements or physical features. For instance, a disabled person may, because of their disability, use a conventional key board less quickly than a non-disabled person. This in itself might not constitute a substantial disadvantage. But if that person was not selected for employment because of performing typewritten tests slower than the successful candidate, this presumably would constitute a substantial disadvantage.

Neither of the terms 'arrangements' nor 'physical feature' is defined in the 1995 Act, but the breadth of these terms is clear from the list of examples of potential adjustments provided in the DDA (see below). The Minister stressed that the term 'arrangements' includes any aspect of selection and interview procedures, job offers, contractual arrangements, or working conditions (Paice, Hansard, 7 February 1995, 142).

Failure to comply with this duty will not constitute an act of discrimination if the employer can show that it was justified (s. 5(2)(b)), i.e., if it was for a reason which is both material to the circumstances of the case and substantial (s. 5(4)). It is not clear what this adds to the 'reasonableness' standard, i.e., in what circumstance it might be reasonable for an employer to provide an adjustment, but he could nevertheless establish a justification that there was a material and substantial reason for not providing it.

Note that the duty applies only to premises occupied by the employer. Thus, for example, where a travelling salesman is unable to access the premises of important customers of a firm, the employer will not be obliged to adapt those premises. However, the employer would be required to consider other ways of resolving the problem, i.e., by altering the work arrangements to allocate customers with accessible premises to the disabled person.

What is a reasonable adjustment?   The 1995 Act includes an illustrative list of steps which it may be reasonable for an employer to take. These include:

(a)   making adjustments to premises;
(b)   allocating some of the employee's duties to another person;

(c) transferring him or her to an existing vacancy;
(d) altering his or her working hours;
(e) assigning him or her to a different place of work;
(f) allowing time off for rehabilitation, assessment or treatment;
(g) arranging training;
(h) acquiring or modifying equipment;
(i) modifying instructions or reference manuals;
(j) modifying procedures for testing or assessment;
(k) providing a reader or interpreter; and
(l) providing supervision.

(See s. 6(3).)

Many of these steps are common sense. Modifying testing procedures might, for example, entail allowing a person with restricted manual dexterity to take an oral rather than a written test; instructions might need to be conveyed orally rather than in a written form to a person with learning disabilities; a reader may be needed to enable a blind employee to carry out certain functions of the job; additional training or supervision might be required, where a person with learning disabilities starts a new job. Where a person becomes disabled and cannot, even with reasonable adjustment, return to his or her original job, an employer may (depending on the employee resources and other factors) be required to retrain them for another position, as well as allowing time off for rehabilitation.

In determining whether an adjustment is effective (i.e., will enable the disadvantage faced by the disabled employee to be overcome) and is legally required (i.e., would be 'reasonable' under the terms of the Act) it will be helpful first to consult the disabled employee. What is appropriate for one disabled person may not be appropriate for another one with the same impairment. For example, some visually impaired people read braille, while others do not or may prefer to receive taped information in particular circumstances. It may also be appropriate to consult expert advice.

An employer will not necessarily be expected to take any of these steps. He or she will be obliged to take only such steps as are reasonable in all the circumstances. The DDA provides a list of factors which will be taken into account in assessing whether an employer has acted reasonably in refusing an adjustment. These are (s. 6(4)):

(a) *The extent to which the step would prevent the effect in question.* If an adjustment would have little impact in reducing the disadvantage faced by the disabled employee, it is unlikely to be reasonable. Conversely, if there were two alternative adjustments, both equally reasonable in terms of the other factors, it would be reasonable for an employer to provide the most effective adjustment.

(b) *The extent to which it is practicable for the employer to take the step.* This category seems intended to enable considerations other than purely financial ones to be taken into account. For example, if the adjustment consisted of exchanging job duties with another member of staff, this might not be practicable in a small team where consideration needed to be given to the fact that the other employee might be off sick, or on holiday, and no alternative cover could practicably be organised.

(c) *The financial and other costs which would be incurred by the employer in taking the step and the extent to which it would disrupt any of his activities.* The wording of s. 6(4)(c) suggests that as well as the direct cost of the adjustment, indirect costs such as staff time will be taken into account.

(d) *The extent of the employer's financial and other resources.* The wording of s. 6(4)(d) suggests that it is the resources of the employer as a whole, rather than the particular work place or organisational unit within a larger enterprise, that will be taken into account. 'Other resources' would presumably cover the number of staff employed by an employer.

(e) *The availability to the employer of financial or other assistance with respect to taking such a step.* If an outside agency, or indeed the employee, were to provide additional assistance to facilitate the reasonable adjustment, this would be taken into account in determining reasonableness. The prime external source of assistance is the range of support services provided by the statutory Employment Service (see below).

Although the DDA 1995 requires these factors in particular to be taken into account, there may be additional factors which should be considered in determining reasonableness. For example, if the adjustment brought a benefit to the employer over and above that to the disabled employee (for example, installing a lift would benefit all staff, and also customers), this could be taken into account.

Regulations may determine when arrangements or physical features are, or are not, to be taken to have a substantial adverse effect; when employers will be required to take certain prescribed steps; which steps it will always or never be reasonable for an employer to take; and when things are and are not to be treated as physical features (s. 6(8)). In particular, there is scope for the Secretary of State to impose a cost ceiling in relation to this duty (s. 6(9)), although he has indicated that it is not intended to use this power initially (in contrast to the goods and services provision).

Alterations to premises occupied under leases

Section 16 of the DDA 1995 addresses the situation where an employer or trade organisation occupies premises under a lease and, but for this section, the occupier would not be entitled to make a particular alteration to the premises. Where the occupier is required to make such an alteration to comply with their duty to make reasonable adjustments, s. 16(2) modifies the effect of the lease to permit the adjustment provided that the occupier seeks written consent from the lessor. The lessor is not entitled to withhold such a consent unreasonably (s. 16(2)(c)), but is allowed to impose reasonable conditions to the consent (s. 16(2)(d)).

The occupier must apply for consent in writing, and is not able to plead as a defence to a request for reasonable adjustment any constraint imposed by a lease unless this has been done (sch. 4, para. 1). Schedule 4, para. 2 allows an industrial tribunal to join a lessor as a party to proceedings in appropriate circumstances defined in that pargraph. Paragraph 3 creates a power to make regulations as to the circumstances in which a lessor will be taken to have withheld consent unreasonably or reasonably, and when conditions imposed by a lessor will be deemed to be reasonable or unreasonable.

Equivalent provision with regard to service providers is established by s. 27.

What Help does the State Provide?

The Employment Service's Placing Assessment and Counselling Teams (PACTs) provide a specialist support service for disabled people and their employers. Team members, known as Disability Employment Advisers (DEAs), can be contacted through local Job Centres. They provide free advice and assistance. For example, they can arrange for an assessment and rehabilitation programme for a newly disabled employee, and can also advise on appropriate forms of adjustment to enable a disabled employee to work in a specific work place, including advising on technical assistance, and arranging for training where necessary.

Under the Access to Work programme, PACTs provide help for disabled workers to meet additional disability-related costs. This may take the form of adapting a particular work place, providing a piece of specialist equipment, providing a support worker (to provide communication support for employees with a hearing impairment, physical assistance, or a reader for visually impaired persons), assistance with additional travelling expenses or providing a 'job coach' to enable an employee with learning disabilities to be given the additional initial guidance which may be required to perform a particular job.

At present, assistance under the Access to Work scheme is available without any charge to employer or employee, up to an initial £21,000 over a five-year period (more may be made available at the discretion of the Employment Service), to people who qualify for registration under the DP(E)A 1944. However, since the register is abolished by the DDA (see p. 29), new criteria for access to the scheme will have to be devised.

The Department for Education and Employment will be reviewing this and other aspects of the scheme prior to the coming into force of the employment provisions of the DDA 1995.

Case Study

Before going on to examine the different elements of discrimination in more detail, an example will help to illustrate the way in which the new law will work. The example is based on a case brought in the USA under the ADA 1990 (*US EEOC* v *AIC Security Investigations Ltd* [1993] 823 F Supp 571 N.D. Ill.). Although ADA case law must be referred to with great care, because of the substantial difference between it and the DDA 1995, the facts are instructive.

Proceedings were brought on behalf of an executive director of a company, who had been discharged less than four months after being diagnosed as having inoperable brain cancer. In defending the claim, the company argued that the director was unable to perform the essential functions of the job, since regular and predictable attendance was required and the director had been absent for 20 days in the previous four months. However, this was successfully countered by evidence that the director had worked extremely long hours when he was present in the office, that he was able to conduct many of his job functions from home by telephone, and that he had never received any warnings about excessive absenteeism. One of the company's clients testified that he had never had any difficulty reaching the director when he was needed.

The company also argued that the director could not perform his job safely because he refused to give up driving, although his condition posed a threat of seizures which made driving hazardous. However, the company was held not to have shown that driving was an essential part of the job, and in any event had offered to provide the director with a driver, thereby showing that a reasonable accommodation could have eliminated the risk of harm.

Conflicting medical evidence also played a role in the case. However, by failing to arrange a medical examination to determine competence prior to discharging the director, the company had fatally undermined its case. Moreover, the division of the company supervised by the director had significantly outperformed the rest of the company during the period in question. The director was successful, and was awarded a total of $572, 000.

It is possible to glean from this example the typical issues which are likely to be raised in DDA cases, and the types of evidence which will be relevant. The argument did not revolve around whether disability had formed the basis of the decision, as would tend to be the pattern in sex and race cases. Instead, the key issue under the British law would be whether the employer could justify the dismissal as being for a 'material and substantial' reason, and for this purpose the employer would have to show that a reasonable adjustment (in this case allowing flexible hours and work from home, and possibly arranging for a driver) would not have removed such a reason. Evidence as to how the firm made its decision is likely to be crucial — did it discuss the situation with the disabled employee and seek expert advice in an attempt to consider whether reasonable adjustments might be able to resolve any problems? The burden of proof will be on the employer to establish that the decision was justified.

What Forms of Treatment are Prohibited?

Under the DDA 1995, s. 4(1), it is unlawful for an employer to discriminate against a disabled person:

(a)   in the arrangements for appointing employees;
(b)   in the terms on which the employment is offered;
(c)   by refusing to offer the employment.

It is also unlawful for an employer to discriminate against a disabled employee (s. 4(2)):

(a)   in the terms of the employment;
(b)   in the opportunities offered for training, promotion, a transfer or any other benefit;
(c)   by refusing to offer such opportunities;
(d)   by dismissing him or her or subjecting him or her to any other detriment.

These sections are modelled on the equivalent provisions in the sex and race discrimination laws.

Who counts as an employee?

For the purposes of disability discrimination 'employment' is defined either as employment under contract of service or of apprenticeship, or as a contract personally to do any work (s. 68(1)). This means that the 1995 Act will apply not only to employers and employees as commonly understood, but may also apply to self-employed people, if their contracts involve them in carrying out work personally. Thus, for example, a person who works as a home-worker may count either as an employee, or as a self-employed contractor for legal purposes. In either case such a person would be covered by this Act.

'A contract personally to do any work' is a wide and flexible term, the key issue being the extent to which the disabled individual is required to do the work himself or herself. If all or a substantial part of the work could be delegated then the contract is not protected (*Mirror Group Newspapers Ltd* v *Gunning* [1986] IRLR 27, CA).

Generally speaking, employees of the Crown are covered by the employment provisions of the 1995 Act (ss. 64 and 66), although certain occupations are excluded (see below).

Contract workers

Section 12 of the DDA 1995 clarifies the position with regard to contract workers. It makes it illegal for a principal to discriminate against a disabled person in relation to contract work:

(a)   in the terms on which he allows him or her to do that work;
(b)   by not allowing him or her to do it;
(c)   in the way he affords him or her access to benefits;
(d)   by subjecting him or her to any other detriment.

A 'principal' means a person who enters into a contract with another employer to provided him or her with contract workers. The same basic prohibitions against discrimination apply to principals as they apply to employers (s. 12(3)). This provision does not apply to contracts for work outside Great Britain.

For example, a disabled caterer is employed by Temps Ltd. Temps provide the caterers to Hotel Ltd. Temps are still the caterer's employer. Provided they have 20 or more employees, Temps cannot discriminate against the caterer. Section 12 means that in addition, if the hotel discriminate against the disabled caterer this will also be illegal. Indeed, a person working for a small business with less than 20 employees may be protected against discrimination by their 'host' workplace (in this case the local authority) but not by their own employer.

If a reasonable adjustment is required to the host work environment, then it may be the duty of the host (i.e., the hotel) rather than the employer (i.e., Temps) to provide that adjustment. It may be difficult to determine whether a particular reasonable adjustment falls to the host rather than the employer, and it is hoped that the Code of Practice may give some indications in this area.

What if the discrimination is by a fellow employee?

Employers are legally responsible for any acts of discrimination carried out by their employees in the course of their employment, whether or not it was done with their knowledge or approval (DDA 1995, s. 58). An employer will, for example, be responsible for a medical officer who rejects a disabled applicant without considering the possibility of reasonable adjustment, and also for employees harassing a colleague.

The only circumstance in which an employer will not be liable in this way is where it can be shown that the employer has taken 'such steps as were reasonably practicable' to prevent his or her employees doing such acts (s. 58(5)).

The individual employee who has performed the act of discrimination is also legally liable, and proceedings can be brought against both employer and employee.

What is meant by 'arrangements'?

The broad term 'arrangements' has deliberately been used ... to cover anything done by or for an employer as part of his recruitment process or in making available opportunities in employment. (Paice, Hansard, 7 February 1995, 142.)

The term will thus include any aspect of selection and interview procedures, job offers, contractual arrangements, or working conditions. However, advertisements are dealt with in a separate section (see p. 30 below).

What count as benefits?

The term 'benefit' in s. 4(2)(b) of the 1995 Act includes any facilities and services provided by, or on behalf of, an employer. The sole exception is those services which are not materially different from those offered to members of the public (s. 4(3)). These would be covered instead by Part III of the Act, relating to goods and services generally. For example, if a disabled person works for a hotel chain which gives its employees reduced rates, and the disabled person is not offered the same reduction, this will be discriminatory (unless the employer can justify it). But if there is no special reduction and the disabled person is discriminated against when visiting a hotel as a member of the public, this issue would need to be taken up under Part III.

The term 'benefit' includes not only those facilities provided directly by an employer (company cars, cafeteria, preferential loans etc.), but also those provided by others to which that employer has the power to give access. For example, if a disabled person works for a travel agency which has an arrangement with certain hotels to give its employees reduced rates, and if the disabled person is not offered the same reduction, this will be discriminatory (unless the employer can justify it).

One of the most significant benefits provided to employees is their occupational pension, and s. 17 addresses this issue. It imposes a non-discrimination rule into occupational pension schemes. This makes it a breach of the rules of a scheme for the trustees to discriminate in connection with the provision of a pension scheme to employees. What will count as unjustifiably less favourable treatment in this context is likely to be a complex issue, which will almost certainly be the subject of specific regulations under the power in s. 17(3).

The arrangement of insurance by an employer to provide benefits for employees (for example, medical insurance) is an increasingly important 'perk'. This type of benefit is specifically addressed by s. 18. This allows complaints against an insurance company in these circumstances to be brought before an industrial tribunal (rather than in a county court as in Part III). This allows a disabled employee to make a complaint against the employer and the insurance company at the same time, if necessary.

What is meant by 'any other detriment'?

'Detriment' (see s. 4(2)(d)) has not been defined in the DDA, or in the previous anti-discrimination statutes in which it is also used. It is very much a catch-all phrase which has been defined as any action 'putting at a disadvantage' (*Jeremiah* v *Ministry of Defence* [1979] IRLR 436, CA). To show a detriment, a tribunal will need to be convinced that the reasonable worker would have been disadvantaged in the circumstances in which he or she had to work, as a result of the actions complained about (*De souza* v *Automobile Association* [1986] IRLR 103, CA). This might include, for example, having to work in unpleasant conditions, receiving a formal warning, demotion or transfer to a less interesting area of work.

Is harassment unlawful?

Although there is not a separate section in the 1995 Act which relates to harassment, litigation under the SDA 1975 established that harassment can constitute less favourable treatment to the employee's detriment (*Strathclyde Regional Council* v *Porcelli* [1986] IRLR 134, CS). The same principles would apply to the DDA, so that if a disabled person was harassed for a reason related to his or her disability, and this resulted in a 'detriment', this would constitute unlawful discrimination.

The first question is whether something has happened as a result of the harassment which is to the employee's detriment. If a person is sacked or resigns because of harassment on the basis of disability then this clearly is to his or her 'detriment'. If there is no particular detriment apart from the harassment itself, then this will constitute discrimination if a reasonable disabled worker in the same situation would or might have taken the view that he or she had been put at a disadvantage in the circumstances in which he or she had to work.

The other issue which arises is whether the treatment complained of was on the basis of disability. Sex discrimination cases have established that even if an equally disliked male would have been equally badly treated, if the weapon used was related to the individual's sex this would constitute sexual harassment (*Strathclyde Regional Council* v *Porcelli* [1986] IRLR 134, CS). The same principle would apply to disabled people.

Exclusions

Significant sections of the workforce will be excluded entirely from the provisions of Part II of the DDA, by virtue of the nature of their employment or size of their employer's business. (Note that these exclusions apply only to Part II of the Act. Small firms, for example, will be covered by the provisions relating to goods and services in Part III.)

Small businesses

The employment provisions of the DDA do not apply to employers with fewer than 20 employees (s. 7). Whether or not the relevant numbers of employees are employed is determined at the time of the alleged act of discrimination.

For this purpose the term 'employees' includes all those who fall within the definition of 'employment' (s. 68(1)), whether or not, for example, they work part-time. All of the employees employed by a particular employer are taken into account for this purpose, regardless, for example, of whether they are scattered over a number of work places.

The Secretary of State has the power to lower the size of exempt firms by order (s. 7(2)). If he has not conducted a review prior to the fourth anniversary of the coming into force of the section, the Secretary of State will be required to review the exclusion on that date (s. 7(5)). If he wishes to reduce or remove the exclusion prior to this, he must conduct a formal review as set out in the Act (s. 7(4)).

Work abroad

Work performed wholly or mainly outside Britain is excluded (ss. 4(6) and 68(2)).

Employment on ships, aircraft and hovercraft

Except in prescribed cases, work on board a ship, aircraft or hovercraft is also exempt from the employment provisions of the DDA (s. 68(3)).

Partnerships

Although both the SDA 1975 and RRA 1976 contain specific provisions making discrimination against partners unlawful, partners are not covered by the DDA 1995. The Minister argued that he was unconvinced that this was an area in which disabled people experienced discrimination, or that legislation was the best way to prevent it (Lord Mackay, Hansard, 13 June 1995, 1782). This omission is likely to affect professional disabled people in particular.

Armed services

All members of the police forces (including, for example, British Transport Police), and armed services (naval, military or air), and prison officers and members of a fire brigade if they may be required to engage in fire fighting, are excluded from the employment provisions of the 1995 Act (s. 64).

Code of Practice

The employment provisions (Part II) of the DDA will be brought into force probably toward the end of 1996. The Government has indicated that, prior to this, it will introduce a Code of Practice (under the power in s. 53). Such a Code will contain practical guidance with a view to the elimination of discrimination against disabled people in the field of employment and encouraging good practice.

In particular, the Act provides that a code may include practical guidance as to the circumstances in which, having regard to the costs, a person might be expected to make reasonable adjustments for a person with a disability, or what steps an employer may be expected to take to prevent employees performing discriminatory acts, for which the employer would otherwise be vicariously liable (s. 53(3)). Although the Act does not specifically single out this issue, the code may also be expected to provide some vitally needed explanations as to which reasons might count as 'material and substantial' from the point of view of establishing a defence to discrimination.

As with the SDA 1975 and RRA 1976, a failure on the part of an employer to observe the provisions of a Code does not in itself constitute discrimination (s. 53(4)). However, where proceedings have been brought for an alleged act of discrimination, and any provision of the Code appears to a tribunal to be relevant to any question, it will be taken into account (s. 53(6)). In practice tribunals have placed a great deal of reliance on the Codes of Practice issued under the SDA 1975 and RRA 1976.

Disabled Persons (Employment) Act 1944

Prior to the DDA, the DP(E)A 1944 was the key legislation regulating the employment of disabled workers. Substantial sections of this Act will be repealed when the DDA 1995 employment provisions come into force.

Registration

The DP(E)A 1944 established a register of workers who were 'occupationally handicapped'. This register was divided into two parts — those who were capable of normal or open employment, and those who could work only in 'sheltered' or 'supported' employment. This register will be abolished (DDA 1995, s. 61(7)(b)).

Open employment With regard to 'open' employment, the DP(E)A 1944 imposed certain requirements on employers with 20 or more employees, designed to promote the employment of a 'quota' of registered disabled employees (set at 3 per cent of the workforce). These requirements, governing the appointment and dismissal of registered disabled employees, have been repealed (DDA 1995, s. 61(7)(c)).

The provisions reserving certain jobs for registered disabled employees will also be repealed (DDA 1995, s. 61(7)(d)).

Supported employment The provisions of the DP(E)A 1944 regarding supported employment have been retained. For disabled people whose productivity is sufficiently impeded that they are unable to gain or hold jobs competitively, the system of supported employment will continue to apply as before.

Around 13,000 disabled people are currently employed in supported workshops — organisations producing goods and services whose prime goal is to provide jobs for less productive disabled people. A further 9,000 disabled people work in mainstream jobs, but receive additional support from the state — generally in the form of subsidies to their employers to compensate for lower productivity.

The 1995 Act introduces only two differences with regard to supported employment. First, the abolition of the register means that a new system for identifying individuals eligible for supported employment must be devised. Secondly, private companies will in future be allowed to contract direct with Government for supported employment (DDA 1995, s. 61(3) and (4)).

Advisory bodies

The DP(E)A 1944 established a national body whose role it is to advise the Secretary of State on matters connected with the employment and training of disabled people — the National Advisory Council on the Employment of People with Disabilities

(NACEPD). NACEPD remains in existence, and will give advice on the operation of the employment provisions of the DDA 1995. Like the National Disability Council, which performs a similar role for the remaining provisions of the Act, the NACEPD has no power to take enforcement proceedings or to provide advice to the public.

The 1944 Act also established local advisory committees (Committees on the Employment of People with Disabilities: CEPDs) whose role it is to advise on local employment issues, including performing certain roles under the quota scheme. These also remain in existence.

However, the DDA 1995 gives the Secretary of State the power to abolish these bodies by order (s. 60(6)), and it seems likely that this power will be used within the next few years. If he does decide to abolish the NACEPD or the CEPDs, the Secretary of State may appoint such local or national advisers on the employment of disabled people as he thinks fit (s. 60). If he does not choose to use this power, responsibility for advice on the employment of disabled people will pass to the National Disability Council by virtue of s. 50(10). There is a strong body of opinion within Parliament that it would be preferable for the National Disability Council to oversee the whole Act.

Other Forms of Employment-Related Discrimination

Advertisements

While publishing a racially or sex discriminatory advertisement is unlawful in itself (with either the CRE or EOC having the power to take proceedings), this is not the case with regard to an advert, no matter how blatant, which discriminates against disabled people.

The DDA 1995 does address the issue of discriminatory advertisements (for employment but not for goods and services), but in a very convoluted and unsatisfactory manner. Section 11 provides that where:

(a)   a disabled person has applied for employment with an employer; and
(b)   the employer has not offered him or her the employment; and
(c)   the disabled person has taken out a complaint against the employer; and
(d)   the employer has advertised the employment; and
(e)   the advertisement indicates, or might reasonably be understood to indicate, either that having any disability (or a disability such as the disabled person in question has) would be a disadvantage, or that the employer would be reluctant to make reasonable adjustments

then the tribunal hearing the complaint will assume, unless the contrary is shown, that the reason why the employer refused the job to the disabled applicant was related to his or her disability.

All that this means is that where a discriminatory advertisement has appeared, and a disabled person does not get the job and lodges a complaint against the employer, then the tribunal will assume, unless shown otherwise, that the decision related to that person's disability.

There are two very obvious problems with this approach. First, it is unlikely that a disabled person would apply for a job after an employer had made it clear that he or she did not welcome disabled applicants. Secondly, even if a tribunal assumes that a decision was based on the disabled person's disability, this will not go very far towards establishing a case of discrimination; the employer can still argue that the decision was justified under the 1995 Act.

Victimisation

Section 55 of the 1995 Act makes it illegal to victimise a person. This provision is closely modelled on the equivalent sections in the sex and race discrimination laws.

'Victimisation' is defined as treating a person less favourably because that person has:

(a)   taken proceedings (against the perpetrator or anyone else) under the DDA; or

(b)   given evidence or information in connection with such proceedings; or

(c)   done something 'by reference to' the DDA, for example complained to the National Disability Council; or

(d)   alleged that someone has breached the DDA;

or because the perpetrator believes or suspects that the 'victim' intends to do one of the above things (DDA 1995, s. 55(1) and (2)).

Note that this is the only section of the Act which applies to non-disabled as well as to disabled people.

Note also that if a person has been treated less favourably because of an allegation which is false *and* which was not made 'in good faith', that person is not able to claim legal protection against such actions (s. 55(4)).

This section closely parallels the provisions of the SDA 1975 and the RRA 1976. The only effective difference is that, in order to determine whether a disabled person has been treated less favourably, that person's disability must be ignored for the purposes of the comparison.

Note that harassment (p. 27) is a different legal issue from victimisation. Harassment is a specific form of less favourable treatment; victimisation (which may take the form of harassment) is less favourable treatment for certain specifically prohibited reasons.

Aiding unlawful acts

A person who knowingly aids another person to do an act made unlawful by the DDA 1995 is treated as if he or she had committed the act of discrimination (s. 57). This is modelled on similar provisions in the other discrimination laws.

A person who is alleged to have aided an act of discrimination in this way will have a defence if he or she had been told that the action was not discriminatory *and* it was reasonable to rely on such a statement (s. 57(3)). A person who makes a statement to the effect that the act which is being assisted is not discriminatory commits an offence, if the statement is false or misleading in a material respect (s. 51(4)).

Trade unions and trade associations

The DDA 1995 makes unlawful discrimination against disabled people by 'trade organisations' (s. 13). The term 'trade organisation' includes trade unions, organisations of employers and organisations whose members carry out a particular profession or trade for the purposes of which the organisation exists (s. 14(4)). This last category would therefore include organisations such as the Bar Council, the Law Society and the British Medical Association.

Such organisations will in any event be covered by the general provisions regarding employees. Section 13 simply means that, in addition, their services to members are required to be non-discriminatory. It is important to note that the definition of discrimination, and in particular the duty to provide reasonable adjustments, follows the model of the employment provisions of the Act rather than the goods and services requirements. Thus, it has been indicated that the reasonable adjustment requirements for providers of goods and services will be subject to a cost limit, but this would not apply to trade organisations. They would be subject to such a limit only if the Secretary of State exercised his powers to impose one under the employment provisions (s. 15(7)).

It is unlawful for a trade organisation to discriminate against a disabled person who wishes to join the organisation, either by rejecting that person's application or by offering membership on less favourable terms (s. 13(1)). Furthermore, it is unlawful for a trade organisation to discriminate against disabled members by denying them access to benefits, depriving them of membership, or providing membership or benefits on less favourable terms (s. 13(2)).

As in other aspects of the 1995 Act, discrimination is defined as less favourable treatment for a reason which relates to a person's disability and failure to comply with a duty to provide reasonable adjustments, which cannot be justified.

Justifying discrimination by a trade organisation   The justifications which are accepted under s. 14 parallel those in the general employment provisions. To justify less favourable treatment a trade organisation must show that the reason for the treatment was both material to the circumstances of the particular case and substantial (s. 14(3) and (4)). If the material reason for less favourable treatment could have been resolved by a reasonable adjustment, then the decision cannot be justified (s. 14(5)).

Regulations may make provision as to the circumstances in which treatment is, or is not, to be justified (s. 14(6)).

Duty to make reasonable adjustments   Where any arrangements made by or on behalf of a trade organisation, or any physical features of premises occupied by such an organisation, place the disabled person at a substantial disadvantage in comparison with persons who are not disabled, the organisation must take such steps as are reasonable under all the circumstances to prevent the disadvantageous effect (s. 15).

The duty is not owed to disabled applicants or members unless the trade organisation knows, or could reasonably be expected to know, that they have a disability and as a result are placed at a substantial disadvantage by the organisation's arrangements or premises (s. 15(5)(b)). Neither does the duty arise toward potential applicants unless they have told the trade organisation that they may apply for membership (s. 15(5)(a)).

Furthermore, as with the employment provisions generally, the duty arises only where a disabled person is placed at a substantial disadvantage, and failure to comply will not constitute discrimination if it is for a substantial, material reason (s. 14(4)).

The 1995 Act also provides a list of factors which will be taken into account in assessing whether a trade organisation has acted reasonably in refusing an adjustment. These are (s. 15(3)):

(a)   the extent to which the step would prevent the effect in question;

(b)   the extent to which it is practicable for the organisation to take the step;

(c)   the financial and other costs which would be incurred by the organisation in taking the step and the extent to which it would disrupt any of its activities;

(d)   the extent of the organisation's financial and other resources;

(e)   the availability to the organisation of financial or other assistance with respect to taking such a step.

Regulations may also be made indicating when arrangements or physical features are, or are not, to be taken to have a substantial adverse effect; when organisations will be required to take certain prescribed steps; which steps it will always or never be reasonable for an organisation to take; and when things are and are not to be treated as physical features (s. 15(7)).

4   Goods and Services

The extent to which the requirements of the DDA 1995 can be extended, restricted or clarified through regulations subsequent to its enactment, makes it difficult to give a clear picture of the scope of the Act's provisions. This is particularly true with regard to Part III of the Act, relating to the provision of goods and services. Many of the crucial terms lack adequate definitions, and the level at which the cost ceiling on the duty to provide reasonable adjustments is set (to be announced in 1996) will crucially determine the effectiveness of the Act in dismantling the environmental obstacles confronting disabled people.

The Codes of Practice which can be drawn up by the National Disability Council, at the request of the Secretary of State (ss. 51 and 52), will also play an important role in clarifying the requirements of Part III. A failure to observe the provisions of a code does not in itself constitute discrimination (s. 51(3)). However, where proceedings have been brought for an alleged act of discrimination, and any provision of the Code appears to a court to be relevant to any question, it will be taken into account (s. 51(5)).

The Government has indicated that the basic right of access to services will be introduced at the end of 1996. It intends to phase in the duty to make adjustments for disabled customers, possibly over a ten-year period. The Government will be consulting on the timing of the introduction of these provisions in 1996.

What is Covered?

Part III of the DDA 1995 prohibits discrimination against disabled people in the provision of services, goods or facilities. This is an extremely broad coverage — it includes services provided by public authorities, as well as those provided by private agencies or individuals. It is irrelevant whether or not there is a charge for the service (s. 19(2)(c)).

A list of examples of the types of activity covered is set out in s. 19(3): communication; information services; hotels and boarding houses; financial and insurance services; entertainment facilities; training; employment agencies; professional services; and the use of any public place. This is a non-exhaustive list, and during Parliamentary debates it was, for example, made clear that legal and health services would be covered.

Exclusions

There are a number of explicit exclusions from the right of access (s. 19(5)). Education (including further and higher education) is excluded, as are transport services. Discrimination in relation to the disposal and management of land and premises is covered in separate provisions (ss. 22–24). These areas are discussed later in this chapter.

Two very important areas of exclusion which are implicit rather than explicit, stem from the fact that the right applies only where goods or services are provided *to the public*. This excludes problems arising from the manufacture of goods. Thus, there is, for example, no requirement that manufacturers provide any instructions for their goods in braille. The only exception is where a manufacturer supplies goods direct to the public, for example, by mail-order. For the same reason, services provided by clubs will also be excluded, unless they are also provided to members of the general public.

A further series of exclusions stems from the fact that the right applies only to disabled people to whom a service is being provided. Thus, for example, witnesses or jurors attending court would not be protected by the right, as they are not regarded as receiving a service but rather as performing a civic duty. A further restriction on the coverage of the Act stems from case law under the RRA 1976. In *Amin* v *Entry Clearance Officer, Bombay* [1983] 2 All ER 864 the House of Lords held that the expression 'provision of goods and facilities and services' in the anti-discrimination statutes applied only to activities analogous to those provided by public undertakings. This excludes many areas of government activity, such as prisons and immigration. It is highly likely that the same restriction will be held to apply to the DDA 1995.

It is nevertheless clear that a disabled parent, whose child is the recipient of a service, will be entitled to receive the same services as are provided to other parents, in a form which is accessible to the disabled parent. Thus, for example, 'where a doctor is treating a young child, he not only provides a service to the child but to his parents as well. That would include such things as provision of information about the child's illness and facilities for the parent to accompany the child' (Lord Mackay, Hansard, 15 June 1995, 1943). The same principle would apply to other carers, where information or a service is normally made available to them in that capacity.

Lastly, as with other provisions of the Act, Part III applies only to the provision of services in the United Kingdom (s. 19(2)(b)).

Note that merely because a company may be exempt from the employment provisions of the Act (because it has fewer than 20 employees), it will not be exempt from the goods and services provisions.

Insurance	The Consultative Document proposed that insurance should be excluded from the right of access to goods and services, but in the event the Government changed its mind, and insurance has been included within the general right of access to goods and services under the Act. The Government has, however, indicated in the White Paper that it intends to bring forward regulations to specify the conditions in which discrimination in this area will be treated as justified under the Act. These would 'recognise the need to distinguish between individuals on the basis of the risks which they seek to insure. Insurers will be allowed to charge higher premiums only to the extent that the extra charge is based on actuarial data or other good reasons' (*Ending Discrimination against Disabled People*, London: HMSO, 1995, p. 24).

What is Discrimination in the Provision of Goods and Services?

Part III of the DDA 1995 sets up a two-pronged definition of 'discrimination' similar to the Part II definition (although with some important differences).

A service provider discriminates if he or she treats a disabled person less favourably for a reason which relates to a person's disability and which cannot be justified under the provisions of the Act (s. 20(1)).

A provider of services also discriminates if he or she fails to provide a disabled person with a reasonable adjustment where required to do so under s. 18 *and* this cannot be justified under the provisions of the Act (s. 20(2)).

Section 16 establishes the circumstances in which discrimination is prohibited. It is unlawful for a service provider to discriminate against a disabled person by:

(a)   refusing service; or

(b)   treating the disabled person less favourably in the standard of service, or in the manner in which it is provided (two different issues); or

(c)   providing the service on less favourable terms.

Where a provider discriminates against a disabled person by failing to comply with a s. 21 duty (reasonable adjustments), the effect of which is to make it impossible or unreasonably difficult for a disabled person to make use of a service, this is also said to be unlawful (s. 19(1)(b)). (This provision, however, seems unnecessarily to duplicate the requirement for adjustment which is already contained in the core definition of discrimination.)

Justifications for discrimination

Section 20(3) and (4) of the 1995 Act set out the ways in which a provider of services can justify treatment which would otherwise be discriminatory.

If the treatment is necessary in order not to endanger the health or safety of any person (including the disabled person)   The excuse that disabled people represent some form of a fire hazard has in the past frequently been used by providers of services to justify their exclusion. In some instances the issue is not a genuine one, being used as a pretext or out of ignorance. Even where there is a genuine safety problem, a provider would not normally resort to turning away a customer, but instead would try to devise a solution to enable the customer to remain in safety.

Prior to invoking the justification of health and safety in future, a provider would have to show that there was an objective basis for believing that it applied, and where a genuine problem did arise, would have to consider whether it could be resolved through the reasonable adjustment of management procedures, or premises or the provision of an auxiliary aid.

If the disabled person is incapable of giving informed consent or of entering into an enforceable agreement and for that reason the treatment is reasonable in that case   There is a legal presumption that an adult is capable of entering into an enforceable agreement unless proved otherwise. There is no one legal test which can be applied to determine a person's legal capacity; it will depend upon the nature and complexity of the contract in question. Thus, a person may not be able to understand a complex mortgage arrangement but will be perfectly capable of deciding whether to buy a cup of coffee.

A 'functional' approach to capacity is that adopted by most tests in English law (*Hunter* v *Edney* (1885) 10 PD 93). This entails assessing a person's ability to understand the essential elements of a decision, its nature and effects, and his or her ability to exercise a choice. It does not involve a judgment on the wisdom of the decision.

The DDA 1995 requires a refusal to be reasonable in the circumstances of each distinct case. The Minister clarified:

> It will not be reasonable for service providers to cite this justification when the purchase of a product or service would not normally be the subject of a written agreement. For example, it cannot be used in relation to buying groceries in a supermarket. The subsection will apply only to major purchases — a motor car perhaps — or credit agreements, and it is meant to apply only in a few cases. (Hague, Hansard, 21 February 1995, 350.)

The term 'informed consent' is usually applied in the context of medical treatment. It means that the patient, in order to give full consent to any proposed treatment, must understand in broad terms what the treatment will involve. As with capacity, the question of informed consent depends on the nature of the treatment proposed.

Regulations can be made disallowing this defence where a person is acting for the disabled person under a power of attorney or as a receiver appointed by the Court of Protection, or in Scotland by a curator bonis, tutor or judicial factor (s. 20(7)).

Where a person has been refused treatment, this must be necessary because the provider of services would otherwise be unable to provide the service to members of the public This is intended to be the most difficult justification to evoke:

> It applies only in circumstances in which, if a service provider were to serve a particular disabled person, he would not be able to continue to provide his service at all. (Hague, Hansard, 21 February 1995, 354.)

The Minister provided examples of when such a defence would and would not be established. A cinema could not use the irritation or extra effort required to provide access as an excuse to exclude a disabled person. It would have to prove that it could not show the film if the disabled person were served. In contrast, a coach of champion able-bodied athletes could legally refuse to take on a disabled athlete, if doing so would fundamentally disrupt the service provided.

Where a person has been treated less favourably in the standard, manner or terms on which the service is provided, this must be necessary in order to provide the service either to the disabled person or to other members of the public An example where this justification might be successfully invoked is where a disabled person is attending a concert, and their behaviour would disturb the other concert goers. In this circumstance it might be justifiable for the management to insist that the disabled person takes a particular seat to minimize the disturbance to other customers.

Where there is a difference in the terms in which the service is provided to disabled people, this must reflect the greater cost to the provider It will not always be acceptable for a service provider to pass on higher costs to a disabled customer. It is not permissible to pass on additional costs where these arise out of the provider's compliance with his or her duty to make reasonable adjustments (s. 20(5)).

In contrast, it is permissible for a business to pass on additional costs which arise out of providing a disabled customer with a specialised service, for example, a shoemaker who is asked by a disabled person to make a shoe to an unusual pattern or using an unusual fabric. If the task takes longer than usual or requires a special order, this would amount to a different, more specialised service than would usually be provided, and it would be reasonable to charge more. It will be helpful to ask if the provider would do the same for an able-bodied customer.

Scope of the justification defence   These justifications may be used to excuse a failure to provide a reasonable adjustment, as well as a failure to provide equal treatment (s. 20(9)).

Although there is no explicit requirement that when providers seek to justify their behaviour they must first have complied with their duty to make reasonable adjustments, there is an implicit requirement to this effect. If a provider is trying to justify the refusal of a service, or actions which make it unreasonably difficult for a disabled person to receive a service, then the duty to provide reasonable adjustments will apply. Thus, for example, if the owner of a cinema sought to deny a disabled person access, or to insist that he or she bring an able-bodied companion, he or she might seek to justify this less favourable treatment on health and safety grounds. But, prior to denying access or making it unreasonably difficult to receive a service, the provider would have to consider whether a reasonable adjustment could resolve the problem.

In debates the Minister stressed that it was envisaged that the instances when less favourable treatment could be justified would be rare, and that the tests which providers would have to pass in order to evoke one of these defences were 'severe' (Hague, Hansard, 21 February 1995, 354).

Regulations may specify further circumstances in which less favourable treatment will be deemed to be justified (s. 20(7)). It was indicated that this power would be used 'extremely sparingly' (Hague, Hansard, 21 February 1995, 359).

Proof   To establish one of these justifications a provider must show, first, that he or she believed *at the time of the less favourable treatment* that the justification applied and, secondly, that it was reasonable in all the circumstances to have had such an opinion (s. 17(3)).

This means that merely because a service provider cannot prove that one of the justifications in the 1995 Act applied, this will not, in itself, mean that he or she has committed an act of unlawful discrimination. If the provider genuinely believed that one of the justifications applied, then a disabled complainant will have to show that it was unreasonable for the provider to have held this erroneous opinion. Case law for unfair dismissal established that this 'reasonable opinion' standard means that a complainant has to show that no reasonable person would have acted in this way (*British Leyland (UK) v Swift* [1981] IRLR 91).

Note that this standard of proof is considerably easier for providers to meet than the objective standard which applies in the employment provisions. This difference was explained on the basis that 'Service providers often have to take very quick and perhaps less informed decisions when serving someone. So an opinion-based approach seems appropriate' (Lord Mackay, Hansard, 18 July 1995, 119). However, the Minister also stressed that 'Nevertheless, the proper degree of objectivity is imposed because the opinion must be shown to be reasonably held' (Lord Mackay, Hansard, 18 July 1975, 119). A provider would, for instance, be unable to maintain an erroneous judgment in the face of subsequent evidence to the contrary, perhaps offered as part of conciliation (Hague, Hansard, 21 February 1995, 355).

Regulations may also specify when it will and will not be considered reasonable for a provider to hold an opinion that one of the justifications applies (s. 20(6)).

Duty to Make Reasonable Adjustments

Section 18 of the DDA 1995 requires service providers to take *such steps as are reasonable under the circumstances to*:

   (a)   amend policies, procedures and practices (s. 21(1)); and

   (b)   remove or alter physical features, *or* provide a reasonable means of avoiding them *or* provide a reasonable alternative means of delivering the service (s. 21(2));

where such actions are needed because the disabled person would otherwise find it impossible or unreasonably difficult to use the service.

Furthermore, the service provider is under a duty to provide auxiliary aids or services where these would 'facilitate the use by disabled persons of such a service' (s. 18(4)).

No definition is provided in the Act of the various terms used. However, examples of physical features are provided ('for example, one arising from the design or construction of a building or the approach or access to premises': s. 21(2)), as are examples of auxiliary aids or services ('for example, the provision of information on audio tape or of a sign language interpreter': s. 21(4)). Would moving a chair or table in a restaurant, for example, constitute a practice (the arrangement of the furniture)? Would this depend on whether the furniture needed to be removed on a long term basis, or if it was fixed to the floor?

An example of a practice or policy which might need to be altered for a disabled individual, is a requirement that a driving licence be provided as the sole means of identification. If an individual could not comply with this because his or her impairment prevented him or her from driving (for example, epilepsy or visual impairment), then a provider would be required to consider a different form of identification. Similarly, a shop might need to modify a policy permitting only one person at a time to enter a dressing room, if a disabled person needed and asked for an assistant to be allowed in to help him or her.

Regulations may prescribe what things are, and are not, to be regarded as comprising practices, policies or procedures, physical premises and auxiliary aids or services (s. 21(5)). These distinctions will be particularly important, because it has been proposed that the requirements regarding adjustments to policies should be introduced first, followed by those for auxiliary aids, followed by the requirements concerning physical features.

What triggers the duty?

The distinctions discussed above may also be important because it appears that there is a different 'trigger' for auxiliary aids than for the other two types of adjustments.

Auxiliary aids must be considered wherever these would facilitate the use by disabled persons of the service. In contrast, before an adjustment to a policy or to physical features needs to be considered, the existing policy or physical feature has to make it impossible or unreasonably difficult for a disabled person to use the service.

In assessing whether an adjustment is required because a service is being denied, or made unreasonably difficult, the standard of service is taken into account. Thus, a reasonable adjustment will be required where it is impossible or unreasonably difficult for a disabled person to receive *a comparable* service to that which is provided to other people. An example relating to the adjustment of practices and policies was provided by the Minister:

> The dining area of a particular cafe may occupy two rooms. In one, where 80 per cent of the tables are accommodated, the management are happy to admit guide dogs, but in the other room, where diners are entertained by a pianist, a ban on dogs is applied. In this circumstance, it will not be good enough for the proprietor to suggest that, because a blind person is able to use 80 per cent of the cafe, the service is reasonably accessible. He must consider a reasonable adjustment so that the disabled person can use the service to the full. (Lord Mackay, Hansard, 18 July 1995, 267.)

What is required with regard to physical barriers?

The DDA 1995, s. 21(2) allows a provider to respond to physical barriers to access for disabled people in three different ways:

(a)   by removing or altering the physical feature (e.g., installing a ramp or widening a doorway);
(b)   by providing a reasonable means of avoiding the physical barrier (e.g., by making available an alternative entrance to a building); or
(c)   by providing a reasonable alternative means of delivering a service (e.g., providing a home delivery service for goods).

There was some concern that this approach might allow organisations to continue to provide separate, segregated facilities alongside physically inaccessible 'mainstream' services. The issue hinges upon what form of adjustment it is 'reasonable' for a provider to make, and this in turn depends upon whether access constitutes an intrinsic part of the service. Thus, the Minister made it clear that:

> there will be occasions when physical alterations will be the only reasonable solution because physical access to premises is a fundamental attribute of the service.... It would not be reasonable for the proprietor of a cafe to suggest that a take away meal was a suitable alternative to making an adjustment to the lay-out or construction of his premises which would allow disabled people to enter. (Lord Mackay, Hansard, 15 June 1995, 2022.)

He contrasted such a situation with one where such access was not essential to the service on offer, giving the example of a ticket office for plays. Merely because a ramped entrance might not cost an excessive amount to provide, it would not necessarily be the reasonable solution to the problem. If, as an alternative, the ticket agency was to provide a free telephone ordering and mail service, this might solve the problem and benefit others at the same time.

The goal of the adjustment is to achieve a service as far as possible to the same standard as that received by other people:

> For example, under [section 21], a cinema will have to make reasonable provision to allow wheelchair users a degree of choice as to where they sit. But all the seats in a cinema would not have to be moveable to leave space for a wheelchair. Of course this means that a wheelchair user would have less choice than other customers and thus would receive a lower standard of service. *The requirement, however, is to provide access to a service as close as it is reasonably possible to get to the standard normally offered.* (Lord Mackay, Hansard, 18 July 1995, 266-7.) (Emphasis added.)

Moreover, it is clear that the mere fact of physically being able to access equivalent provision, will not in itself be sufficient to comply with the duty. The means of entrance themselves must be reasonable. In the same speech, the Minister stressed that to expect a wheelchair user to have to negotiate the rubbish bins at the back of a restaurant, to be let in through the kitchens, would not be reasonable.

Regulations may prescribe what matters may be taken into account in determining whether it is reasonable to provide a means of avoiding the obstacle or delivering the service by alternative arrangements (s. 21(3)(a)).

What limits are placed on the provider's duty to make adjustments?

The most obvious limit is that adjustments are not required where they are unreasonable. In contrast to the employment provisions, there are no indications in the 1995 Act itself as to what factors will be taken into account in determining reasonableness. However, the Act does allow for regulations to spell out in more detail the circumstances in which it will be reasonable for a service provider to take steps of a prescribed description (s. 21(5)(a) and (b)). The Government has already indicated that it intends to use this power to prescribe requirements for automated service provision.

In the absence of regulations, great emphasis will be laid on any relevant provision within a code of practice issued under the Act.

It appears that in determining whether an adjustment is reasonable, considerable emphasis will be placed on financial considerations. In particular, the Secretary of State has the power to establish a financial ceiling on the extent of costs which it is reasonable for a provider to incur in making adjustments (s. 21(7), (8) and (9)). The Government has indicated that it intends to use this power to establish a cost ceiling prior to bringing the reasonable adjustment requirement into force (in contrast to the employment provisions, where the equivalent power will be held in reserve). A consultation process will establish how this financial ceiling will be calculated (e.g., a proportion of profits or rateable value; on an annual or five yearly basis; applied to each separate branch of an organisation or to the organisation as a whole?). A separate cost limit can be applied to particular services or particular types of premises.

Adjustments which are reasonable, and would otherwise be required, will not be required if one of the justifications set out in s. 20 applies. For example, a ramp would not be required if in those circumstances it caused a health and safety risk.

Nothing requires a service provider to take steps which would fundamentally alter the nature of the service or business (s. 21(6)). The example given in the White Paper (*Ending Discrimination against Disabled People*, London: HMSO, 1995, p.23) related to a visually impaired person visiting a night club. Although the cost of turning up the lights to improve visibility would be insignificant, because this adjustment would have a fundamental impact on the nature of the business it would not be required. Similarly, where the purpose of an organisation is to provide services to individuals selected on the basis of their physical or mental attributes (for example, a charity specifically providing services to deaf people), then it will not be unlawful for them to operate on this basis. (Section 10, which exempts charities from the employment provisions, has no direct equivalent in Part III, but is not needed because s. 21(6) performs the same role.)

The duty is owed to individual disabled customers when they make use of services. There is no requirement for an organisation to take pre-emptive measures.

Lastly, regulations may exclude certain categories of providers from the aspect of this duty which relates to physical features (s. 21(3)(b)).

Interaction with other Legislation

Statutory authority

By virtue of the DDA 1995, s. 53, anything which is done 'in pursuance of' an Act of Parliament (or an instrument made or approved by Parliament under such an Act) will be lawful, even if it would otherwise amount to discrimination. This applies whether the Act or instrument was passed before or after the DDA 1995. This provision parallels that within the RRA 1976, although the situation with regard to sex discrimination is different because of the operation of European law.

Case law under the RRA 1976 has established that the phrase 'in pursuance of' applies only to actions taken in *the necessary* performance of an *express obligation* contained in an Act or instrument, and does not also include actions which are the exercise of a *power* or *discretion* under legislation (*Hampson* v *Department of Education and Science* [1990] IRLR 302, HL).

Such actions would potentially be covered by the DDA, statutory authority would not form a defence. Thus, where an authority has discretion in the performance of its functions under statutory authority it must exercise that discretion in a non-discriminatory fashion. One case under the RRA 1976 involved the General Medical Council, which under the Medical Act 1983 has the power to determine the registration of persons qualifying overseas. A doctor from India alleged that the process which the Council used for determining registration was racially discriminatory. The Council claimed that its actions in this area fell under the exclusion for statutory acts. The Employment Appeal Tribunal held that this defence did not apply, since it would apply only to acts which were 'reasonably necessary in order to comply with any condition or requirement of the statute or order' (*General Medical Council* v *Goba* [1988] IRLR 425, EAT).

Historic buildings

The requirement to obtain consent for building work carried out on a listed building is one example of a potential conflict between the requirements of the DDA 1995 and other statutory provisions. The Town and Planning Country Acts, as consolidated by the Planning (Listed Buildings and Conservation Areas) Act 1990, establish the criteria for granting listed building consent for alterations. The general standard is that 'special regard' shall be had to 'the desirability of preserving the building or its setting or any feature of special architectural or historic interest' (Planning (Listed Buildings and Conservation Areas) Act 1990, s. 16(2)).

As with other areas of potential conflict, merely because in the final analysis the historic building requirements take precedence over the DDA, this will not mean that an organisation operating from a listed building will be exempt from the DDA requirements. Providers must attempt to meet both sets of requirements. English Heritage is currently producing guidance on how to approach proposals for making historic buildings and monuments more accessible to disabled people; such guidance might be referred to within the Code of Practice to be issued by the NDC (see p. 59).

Even where it is not possible to remove or alter a physical barrier, a provider will need to consider providing a reasonable means of avoiding the barrier, or making the service available in other ways. Where a service is provided from an historic building, and it is not possible to make it accessible without disproportionate harm to the fabric of the building, it might still be possible to situate the service in alternative premises, or make it available by other means. It would not, for example, be appropriate to install a lift into Anne Hathaway's cottage, as to do so would destroy the atmosphere for everyone. Providing an audio visual display of the contents of the upstairs rooms would be an alternative way of enabling disabled visitors to enjoy the function of the building — to share the experience.

Building Regulations

Part M of the Building Regulations has, since 1988, set out the access features needed by disabled people which new non-domestic buildings (and most extensions) are required to provide. They relate to access to the various parts of the building, provision of toilets and, if relevant, audience and spectator seating.

The Disability Discrimination Bill originally exempted buildings constructed in compliance with these regulations from the duty of reasonable adjustment with regard to premises. However, the Government withdrew these clauses, indicating that they were considered too blunt an approach. It has nevertheless said that it will be consulting on how to use the regulation-making power in s. 21(5) to address the overlap between the DDA requirements and those of the Building Regulations, with a view to protecting service providers from 'double jeopardy'.

Purchase or Rental of Premises

What forms of property are covered?

The DDA 1995, ss. 22 and 24 make discrimination in the disposal or management of premises illegal. The term 'disposal' includes the sale or letting of property, and the assignment or sub-letting of premises (s. 22(6)). Land and business properties are covered, as well as residential properties.

Discrimination in the provision of accommodation in hotels, hostels and boarding houses is covered by the main goods and services provision described above (s. 19(3)(d)).

The Act applies to tenancies created before as well as after the Act, but applies only to premises in the United Kingdom (s. 22(8)).

What forms of behaviour are unlawful?

It is unlawful for a person *disposing* of premises to discriminate against a disabled person:

(a) by refusing to dispose of them to the disabled person;
(b) by offering them on worse terms to the disabled person; or
(c) in his treatment of the disabled person in relation to any list of persons in need of premises of that description (s. 22(1)). (Paragraph (c) will cover letting agencies, or council housing lists.)

It is unlawful for a person *managing* premises to discriminate against a disabled person occupying premises:

(a) in the way he or she allows that person to make use of any benefits or facilities;
(b) by refusing that person the use of such benefits or facilities;
(c) by evicting that person or subjecting him or her to any detriment (s. 22(3)).

It is unlawful for a person whose consent is required for the disposal of any property (for example, the assignment of a lease) to discriminate against a disabled person by withholding that consent (s. 22(4)).

This list of proscribed actions closely parallels the provisions of the sex and race discrimination Acts, as does the list of excluded premises set out below. However, the meaning of 'discrimination' differs from those Acts, following the pattern of other sections of the DDA, with one notable exception — there is no duty to provide reasonable adjustments.

Discrimination for the purposes of s. 22 is defined as less favourable treatment for a reason which relates to the person's disability, which cannot be justified under the Act (s. 24(1)).

Justifications for discrimination

The permissible justifications with regard to less favourable treatment in the disposal or management of premises are essentially the same as in the general goods and services provisions. Section 24(3) provides that less favourable treatment is justified if:

(a) the treatment is necessary in order not to endanger the health or safety of any person (including the disabled person);

(b)   the disabled person is incapable of giving informed consent or entering into an enforceable agreement, and for that reason the treatment is reasonable in that case;

(c)   where a person has received less favourable treatment in using the facilities, the treatment is necessary in order for the disabled person or occupiers of other premises forming part of the same building to make use of the benefit or facility;

(d)   where a person has been refused the use of facilities, this is necessary in order for the occupiers of other premises forming part of the same building to make use of the benefit or facility.

Regulations may specify further circumstances in which less favourable treatment will be deemed to be justified (s. 24(5)).

To claim one of these justifications a provider must show, first, that he or she believed *at the time of the less favourable treatment* that the justification applied and, secondly, that it was reasonable in all the circumstances to have had such an opinion (s. 24(2)).

Regulations may also specify when it will and will not be considered reasonable for a provider to hold an opinion that one of the justifications applies (s. 24(4)).

Exclusions

Private sale   The provisions regarding the disposal of property do not apply to an owner-occupier if the sale or letting is a private one, i.e., not through an estate agent or an advertisement (s. 22(2)). However, since even a 'For Sale' sign outside a property counts as an advertisement, such purely private transactions are very rare.

Small dwellings   In relation to any of the prohibited actions, small dwellings which come with very tightly drawn circumstances are exempt (s. 23). To be classified as a 'small dwelling' a property must *either* be divided in such a way as to provide accommodation for no more than three households, one of which is occupied by the landlord (s. 23(4)); *or* there must be accommodation on the premises for no more than six persons in addition to the landlord or near relative (s. 23(5)).

Such small premises will be excluded from the DDA if:

(a)   either the landlord, or a near relative, lives on the premises and intends to continue doing so; and

(b)   the landlord, or near relative, has to share certain accommodation with the other people living there. The shared accommodation must be something other than a common entrance hall or staircase or storage accommodation. It might, for example, be a kitchen, bathroom or lavatory.

If a building comes within the definition of a 'small dwelling' and meets the other two conditions, then its landlord can freely discriminate, as he or she will be excluded from the provisions of the 1995 Act. For example, the owner of a building has a daughter who lives in a flat at the top of that building. There are three other flats available for rent. All four flats share a toilet. In these circumstances it will not be unlawful for the owner to refuse to rent one of the flats to a person because, for example, that person has a learning disability.

Void Contract Terms

Section 26 of the 1995 Act provides that any term in a contract for the provision of goods, facilities or services, or in any other agreement, is void in so far as it purports to:

(a)   require a person to do anything which would contravene any provision of Part III of the Act;

(b)   exclude or limit the operation of any provision of Part III;

(c)   prevent any person from making a claim under Part III.

Points (b) and (c) do not, however, apply to agreements settling a claim under s. 25 of the Act (s. 26(2)).

On application, a county court (or a sheriff court in Scotland) can make such an order as it thinks just for removing or modifying such a term (s. 26(3)).

See p. 22 for the legal position where the terms of a lease prevent a provider making a reasonable adjustment.

Employer's Liability

Employers are legally responsible for any acts of discrimination carried out by their employees in the course of their employment, whether or not done with their knowledge or approval (s. 58). (See pp. 25–6 above.)

Victimisation

Section 55 of the DDA 1995 makes it illegal to victimise a person. (See p. 31 above.)

Aiding Unlawful Acts

A person who knowingly aids another person to do an act made unlawful by the DDA 1995 is treated as if he or she had committed the act of discrimination (s. 57). (See p. 31 above.)

Part IV   Education

There is still no legislation which prevents discrimination in the provision of education. Education is excluded from the new right of access to goods and services contained in Part III of the DDA.

Training, however, is covered by Part III of the 1995 Act. The distinction relates to the institutional framework in which it is provided. Training which is provided under s. 2 of the Training and Employment Act 1973 (for example, by Training and Enterprise Councils, or Local Enterprise Councils in Scotland) is covered (DDA 1995, s. 19(3)(g)). Education which is funded by or provided by schools, local education authorities (and their Scottish equivalents), the Further Education Funding Councils or the Higher Education Funding Councils, Teacher Training Agency and voluntary organisations is not covered. Where a Training and Enterprise Council funds training which is provided by a voluntary organisation (or another excluded educational body), it must seek to comply with its duties under the Act, even though the direct provider is exempt (s. 19(5)).

In addition, it is important to note that educational institutions will be required to comply with the legislation as regards their employment practices, and with regard to any non-educational provision offered to the public, such as holiday or conference accommodation, or public meeting spaces.

Although teacher training is excluded from coverage by the DDA, an amendment to s. 1 of the Education Act 1994 requires the Teacher Training Agency to have regard to the requirements of disabled people (DDA 1995, s. 29(3)).

Schools

The Education Act 1993 places a duty on all county, voluntary and grant maintained schools to include information relating to pupils with special educational needs in their annual reports. Section 29 of the DDA inserts a new s. 161(6) into the Education Act 1993, creating an additional requirement that such reports must contain specific information regarding:

(a) arrangements made for the admission of disabled pupils;
(b) steps taken to prevent disabled pupils from being treated less favourably than other pupils; and
(c) facilities provided to assist access to the school by disabled pupils.

Although this amendment does not require schools to make their premises accessible, they will at least be required to address the issue. The new provision should assist parents of disabled children in making an informed choice about the education of their children.

Further education

England and Wales Section 30 of the DDA introduces three new elements with regard to the provision of further education in England and Wales. First, it amends the Further and Higher Education Act 1992 by inserting a new s. 5(7A) which requires institutions receiving funding from the Further Education Funding Council to produce 'disability statements' containing prescribed information about their provision of facilities for disabled students. The content and frequency of these statements will be determined by regulations.

Information is likely to include physical access, the provision of specialist equipment, facilities which may help students with particular disabilities, admission policies, counselling and welfare arrangements. (Lord Mackay, Hansard, 15 June 1995, 1991.)

Colleges will be required to produce these statements as a condition of receiving any funding from the funding councils.

Secondly, councils are given the power to require a college to make certain provision for disabled students. The Minister indicated that this might be used if a student made a complaint: 'In future, students who have exhausted their college's internal procedures will be able to seek redress from the councils on the occasions when provision fails to meet expectations raised by the college's disability statement.' (Lord Mackay, Hansard, 18 July 1995, 247.)

Thirdly, the further education councils for England and Wales will be required to report annually to their Secretaries of State detailing progress made during the year with regards to the provision of facilities for disabled students, together with changes planned for the following year (Further and Higher Education Act 1992, s. 8(6), inserted by DDA 1995, s. 30(4)).

Scotland   In Scotland there is no funding council for further education and the existing duties of colleges are also slightly different from those in England and Wales.

Colleges are already required by statute to submit development plans which include information on the provision made for students with learning difficulties and disabilities. This information is used by the Secretary of State in preparing his annual report to Parliament. Ministers propose in future to make it a condition of grant-in-aid that information on such provisions for students on special programmes and students receiving extended learning support be included in the annual reports that colleges are required to produce (Lord Mackay, Hansard, 15 June 1995, 1991).

This arrangement should provide a framework for strategic action very similar to that which the disability statements and annual reporting systems offer in England and Wales.

As with schools, the new provision falls far short of requiring institutions to become accessible. It does, however, improve the provision of information, and should help focus colleges' attention on improvements in this area. It will also increase the power and duty of the funding councils to act strategically to promote the position of disabled students.

Higher education

The DDA 1995 introduces two new duties to the higher education councils in England and Wales, and Scotland. By inserting s. 62(7A) into s. 62 of the Further and Higher Education Act 1992, it creates a new requirement that higher education funding councils in England and Wales must 'have regard to the requirements of disabled persons' (DDA 1995, s. 30(5)).

In addition, institutions receiving funding from such councils will be required to produce regular statements about the provision of facilities for disabled students (Further and Higher Education Act 1992, s. 65(4A), as inserted into s. 65 by DDA 1995, s. 30(6)).

Equivalent provisions for Scotland are introduced into ss. 37 and 40 of the Further and Higher Education (Scotland) Act 1992 (DDA 1995, s. 31).

Northern Ireland

Schedule 8 of the DDA 1995 explains how the Act will effect Northern Ireland. The amendments on further and higher education will not, however, apply to Northern Ireland because the structures to which Part IV refers do not exist there.

Ministers will, however, consider the proposed further education amendments when detailed legislation is being prepared for the incorporation of further education colleges in Northern Ireland:

The FE and HE charters for Northern Ireland, which will be published later this year, will contain a requirement for colleges to make available information on disabled access. Existing powers will permit the Secretary of State to attach conditions to the payment of a grant, and it is his intention to do so. (Lord Mackay, Hansard, 15 June 1995, 1992.)

Part V   Transport

Although 'any service so far as it consists of the use of any means of transport' is exempt from the anti-discrimination provisions contained in Part III of the Act (s. 19(5)(b)), this does not mean that the DDA 1995 will not have a significant impact on transport.

The infrastructure of transportation is covered by the new access right:

The new right of access will apply to stations. The duties in [section 18] must be complied with and policies that make it impossible or unreasonably difficult for disabled people to use stations must be changed, provided that it is reasonable. (William Hague, Hansard, 21 February 1995, 337.)

As an illustration of the sort of issue which would need to be addressed within this duty, the impact of unmanned stations was mentioned.

In addition, Part V of the 1995 Act is devoted entirely to accessibility requirements for public transport vehicles. Specific provisions cover taxis, public service vehicles and rail vehicles. The Secretary of State is given the power to establish minimum access criteria for new public transport vehicles, which can be phased in over a period of time. These provisions are cast in the form of administrative regulations, rather than an individual right of access. The main difference lies in the enforcement mechanisms.

This complicated structure means that individuals who experience problems with transport will have to decide whether or not these relate to the infrastructure, in which case they can bring proceedings in the county court in accordance with the general Part III enforcement provision (see chapter 5), or to a transport vehicle, in which case they must complain to the relevant enforcement body who may bring proceedings if an offence has been committed.

The timetable for introducing the new access requirements has not yet been established. The Act requires the Secretary of State to consult the Disabled Persons Transport Advisory Committee (DPTAC) and any other appropriate organisation prior to making the access regulations.

Taxis

Access standards   The Secretary of State has the power to make regulations defining standards of access which new taxis will be required to meet. The purpose of the regulations is to enable disabled people to get in and out of taxis safely, and to be carried in safety and reasonable comfort (s. 32(1)). The regulations may, in particular, specify the design of taxis and require drivers to carry ramps and secure wheelchairs in a specified manner (s. 32(2)).

It will be an offence for a taxi driver to fail to comply with any such requirement, or to drive a vehicle which fails to conform to the regulations (s. 32(3)). Such an offence is punishable by a fine not exceeding level 3 on the standard scale (s. 32(4)).

These new regulation making powers will only apply to licensed cabs, not private hire cars. However, a new section was added in response to concerns raised about the exclusive contracts awarded to hire cars at key transport facilities, such as Gatwick Airport. If these contracts were awarded to a fleet with no accessible vehicles, this could have a severe impact on disabled travellers. Section 33 gives the Secretary of State a regulation-making power to ensure that when accessibility regulations are in force for taxis generally, equivalent requirements (regarding vehicles and drivers) can be imposed on vehicles used under a contract to provide hire car services at designated transport facilities.

Licensing controls In addition, once the regulations are in force, licensing authorities will not be able to grant licences to taxis unless the vehicles comply with the accessibility provisions (s. 34(1)). To ensure that the phasing in of the new requirements is not too onerous on taxi operators, they will not apply to vehicles which are already licenced as taxis. Even if such vehicles are inaccessible their licence can be renewed (s. 34(2)). However, this exemption for existing taxis will not continue indefinitely. The Secretary of State can establish a date beyond which no non-accessible vehicles can be relicenced (s. 34(3)), and different dates may be set for different parts of the country (s. 34(4)).

Licensing exemptions   Section 35 of the DDA 1995 allows the Secretary of State to grant an order exempting an authority from these licensing restrictions, provided that certain criteria are met. These are that, having regard to the circumstances in its area, it would be inappropriate to apply the access requirements and that the application of such standards would result in an unacceptable reduction in the numbers of taxis in the area (s. 35(3)). A licensing authority wishing to seek such an exemption must carry out prescribed consultations with the local community, publish any proposal in the prescribed manner, consider any representations made before applying for an order and make its application in the prescribed form (s. 35(2)).

On receiving an application from a licensing authority for an exemption, the Secretary of State must consult DPTAC, and such other persons as he considers appropriate. He may then grant or refuse the application, or grant the application on such conditions as he thinks fit (s. 35(4)). Even where an order exempting an area from the full access requirements has been made, the Secretary of State may apply less stringent regulations, requiring the installation of 'swivel seats' (s. 35(5)), and establishing equivalent enforcement mechanisms to those which apply to the full access requirements (s. 35(6)).

Requirement to carry wheelchair users and guide dogs The second set of taxi provisions concern the actions of taxi drivers, as opposed to the design of their vehicles. Section 36 imposes duties on drivers with respect to their treatment of people in wheelchairs (for example, carrying passengers while they remain in their wheelchairs and giving such assistance as is reasonably required to get in and out of the taxi), and s. 37 imposes comparable duties with regard to their treatment of people with guide dogs and hearing dogs (to carry dogs without an additional charge). Any driver failing to comply with these duties commits an offence, punishable by a level 3 fine (s. 36(5) and s. 37(4)).

The s. 36 duty does not require drivers to carry more than one person in a wheelchair on any journey, unless in taxis of a prescribed description (s. 36(4)), or to carry a wheelchair if, despite the taxi complying with all relevant regulations, it would not be safe to do so (s. 36(6)). (This is most likely to apply where a taxi has an exemption from the access requirements by virtue of s. 35.)

There is provision with regard to both these sets of duties for exemption certificates to be issued to a taxi driver (and displayed on the taxi) on medical grounds, for example that a driver has asthma which is exacerbated by proximity to dogs (s. 36(7) and s. 37(5)).

Buses, coaches and other 'public service vehicles'

The DDA 1995, s. 40 gives the Secretary of State the power to make regulations covering access to public service vehicles (PSVs) for disabled people. A PSV is defined in s. 40(5) as a vehicle which is adapted to carry more than eight passengers and which meets the criteria for a public services vehicle established in the Public Passenger Vehicles Act 1981. That definition applies to motor vehicles other than tram cars (which are included within the section on rail vehicles). The purpose of the regulations is to enable disabled people to get on and off buses and coaches in safety, and without unreasonable difficulty, and to be carried in such vehicles in safety and reasonable comfort (s. 40(1)).

Section 40(2) gives a list of the requirements which might be included in such regulations. It is not an exhaustive list, merely highlighting the main issues which would need to be covered, e.g., the fitting of equipment to PSVs, or the equipment to be carried by such vehicles.

Section 40(6) provides for different provisions to be made for different classes or descriptions of vehicles, for the same class operating in different locations, and for different locations. This provision allows regulations to impose different requirements over different time-scales.

Accessibility and approval certificates (the latter to be issued for vehicles produced in large numbers) will be issued by vehicle examiners. Regulations will provide details about the application and inspection procedures (ss. 41 and 42), and an appeal procedure where a certificate is refused (s. 44).

In the absence of such a certificate, a PSV to which the regulations apply will not be permitted to be used on a road. Failure to comply will give rise to an offence with a penalty set at level 4 on the standard scale (s. 40(4)).

There is provision for special operating authorisation to be granted for vehicles which do not conform with the access requirements (s. 43). This is intended to provide 'flexibility to cater for circumstances in which an individual vehicle or class of vehicles cannot reasonably be expected to meet the full requirements of the accessibility requirements' (Lord Mackay, Hansard, 27 June 1995, 717).

Rail

The provisions for rail vehicles are modelled on those concerning PSVs.

The Secretary of State may make regulations defining standards of access to rail vehicles (including light rapid transit and tram systems) to enable disabled people to get on and off in safety and without unreasonable difficulty, and to be carried in such vehicles in safety and reasonable comfort (s. 46).

Section 46(5) provides for different provisions to be made for different classes or descriptions of vehicles, for the same class operating in different locations, and for different networks.

It will be an offence to operate a rail vehicle in public service which does not comply with the accessibility regulations (s. 46(3)), such an offence to be punished by a fine not exceeding level 4 on the standard scale (s. 46(4)).

Section 47 of the DDA 1995 allows the Secretary of State to make exemption orders for vehicles which would otherwise have to comply with the requirements. It was indicated in the House of Lords debate that DPTAC would advise the Secretary of State on such applications, and that it was not envisaged that the power would be widely used (Lord Mackay, Hansard, 27 June 1995, 718).

5   Enforcement

The enforcement procedures and legal remedies established by the DDA 1995 are closely modelled on those applying to the SDA 1975 and RRA 1976. There is, however, one crucial difference from earlier anti-discrimination laws. The DDA 1995 lacks a central enforcement body, comparable to the Equal Opportunities Commission or the Commission for Racial Equality. Instead, the National Disability Council is created. Its members are appointed by the Secretary of State, and its role is solely to advise the Secretary of State on the operation of the Act and on the elimination of discrimination.

The DDA relies for its enforcement entirely on individuals bringing forward cases. The broader enforcement powers of the commissions established under the other anti-discrimination laws (the offences of discriminatory practices and the enforcement mechanisms of investigations and non discrimination notices) have no parallels in this the 1995 Act. Undoubtedly, this is the single greatest weakness in the DDA compared either with the British sex and race statutes, or with comparable legislation in Australia, New Zealand, Canada and the United States, all of which have strategic enforcement agencies.

The employment provisions are enforced through industrial tribunals, and the goods and services provisions through the county courts.

It is worth pointing out that industrial tribunals and courts are themselves covered by the new right of access to goods and services.

Employment

A complaint of unlawful discrimination in relation to employment under the DDA 1995 must be brought in an industrial tribunal (s. 8).

Time limit

Proceedings for disability discrimination must be started within three months of the alleged act of discrimination (sch. 3, para. 3(1)). A course of action which takes place over an extended period of time is treated as having been done at the end of that period (thus, if the term of a contract is the subject of complaint, the act is treated as extending for the duration of that contract). For example, an employer's refusal to provide a mortgage subsidy for an employee was held to be a continuing act of discrimination, up to the time the employee left her employment (*Calder* v *James Finlay Corporation Ltd* [1989] IRLR 55, EAT).

A failure to act will be taken to occur at the time when a decision not to act was taken (sch. 3, para. 3(3)(c)) which, in the absence of evidence to the contrary, will be deemed to be the time at which it would have been reasonable to expect the alleged discriminator to take the required action (sch. 3, para. 4).

The tribunal does have discretion to hear a case, however, even where a complaint has been presented outside the time limit, if it thinks it 'just and equitable to do so' (sch. 3, para. 3(2)). In deciding whether or not to allow an out of time complaint the tribunal may take into account anything which is relevant, including the strength of the case, as well as the reasons for the delay in the application (*Hutchinson* v *Westward Television Ltd* [1977] IRLR 69, EAT).

A tribunal will take into account the possibility that a person's disability has impeded his or her ability to bring the case within the time limit. For example, where a profoundly deaf man had failed to bring his claim for unfair dismissal within the relevant time limit, the tribunal agreed to allow him to pursue his claim. It took into account that 'to a very great extent' the applicant was 'cut off from so many of the informal sources of information which enable other people to learn in a general way of the help and advice open to them' (*Down* v *Emerson Electric Ltd*, COIT 1489/95).

Questionnaires

Both the SDA 1975 and the RRA 1976 contain mechanisms by which people who think that they have been discriminated against in employment can obtain further information from the alleged discriminator. Standard form questionnaires have been issued, through which a complainant can obtain additional information to help decide whether or not to bring a case, and to present such a case in the most effective manner.

The DDA 1995 contains a similar mechanism. Section 56 requires the Secretary of State to produce forms by which the complainant may question the respondent on the respondent's reasons for doing any relevant act (or on any other matter which is or may be relevant), and standard forms in which the respondent may reply to these questions (s. 56(2)).

The Act provides for the setting of time limits within which such questionnaires must be served and responded to (s. 56(4)).

If the alleged discriminator does not reply to questions, or if the replies are evasive or equivocal, the tribunal may draw from this any inference which it considers 'just and equitable'. This might include an inference that the respondent has discriminated unlawfully (s. 56(3)(b)).

Conciliation

As with other employment discrimination claims, the DDA 1995 seeks to encourage parties to a dispute to reach an agreed settlement (sch. 3, para. 1). The Advisory, Conciliation and Arbitration Service (ACAS) will provide a conciliation service free of charge. Anything said or written to conciliation officers cannot be used in evidence at the hearing of a claim, without the consent of the person who said or wrote it (sch. 3, para. 1(4)).

A copy of any complaint lodged with a tribunal will be sent automatically to an ACAS conciliation officer. The officer must try to promote a settlement if it is considered that there is a reasonable prospect of a successful settlement, or if both parties to the case request conciliation (sch. 3, para. 1(1)).

If conciliation is successful, the parties will reach an agreement, which will normally be recorded in writing on the appropriate form. Such an agreement will usually commit the complainant to discontinue the industrial tribunal proceedings, or not to initiate such proceedings in exchange for a sum of money and/or undertakings by an employer to act in certain ways (for example, to offer the complainant the next suitable post or to introduce an equal opportunities policy).

Such ACAS negotiated settlements will not be affected by the provision of the DDA 1995 which treats as void any term of an agreement which purports to prevent a person presenting a complaint under Part II of the Act (s. 9). The general object of this provision is to prevent employers placing undue pressure on potential complainants to waive their right to take legal action.

As well as allowing for binding settlements to be reached with the assistance of ACAS (s. 9(2)(a)), the 1995 Act also allows such agreements to be reached where the potential complainant receives adequate legal advice about the terms and effect of the agreement (s. 9(2)(b)). Section 9(1)(b) and (c) will not apply to agreements where the complainant has received 'independent' legal advice from a qualified lawyer and the following conditions are satisfied:

(a) The advice must be independent, in the sense that it must be given by a lawyer who is not acting for the other party in proceedings, or a company controlled by that other party.

(b) The lawyer must be insured to cover a claim for negligent advice to enter such an agreement.

(c) The agreement must be in writing, and must state that the conditions for a valid binding agreement have been complied with, identifying the particular complaint and the legal adviser (s. 9(3)).

Proof

Complainants must satisfy the tribunal on a balance of probabilities (i.e., that it is more probable than not) that they have been unlawfully discriminated against. However, tribunals in discrimination cases have recognised that it is unusual to find direct evidence of discrimination. The outcome of the case will therefore usually depend on inferences drawn by a tribunal. In cases where there are no obvious nondiscriminatory grounds for the non-appointment or failure to promote a disabled individual, a tribunal is entitled to look to the employer for an explanation. If no explanation is put forward, or if the explanation is unsatisfactory, it is legitimate for a tribunal to infer that the discrimination was on prohibited grounds and thus unlawful (*King* v *The Great Britain-China Centre* [1991] IRLR 513, CA). In addition, tribunals may draw similar inferences from inadequate responses to a questionnaire.

Where employers are seeking to justify unequal treatment the onus of proof will then be on them to show that their reason falls within s. 5.

Remedies

Where a claim for employment discrimination is successful the tribunal may make such orders as it considers 'just and equitable' (s. 8). The orders which may be made are similar to those available in cases of sex or race discrimination.

Compensation   A tribunal may order a respondent to pay compensation (financial damages) to the complainant. The amount of compensation to be awarded will generally follow the principles established by the SDA 1975 and RRA 1976.

Compensation is awarded for foreseeable damages arising directly from an unlawful act of discrimination. A complainant may claim for any pecuniary loss which could properly be attributed to an unlawful act of discrimination. At the same time, however, complainants have a duty to 'mitigate' their losses, that is to take reasonable actions to reduce the amount of loss which they suffer. Thus, if compensation is claimed for loss of earnings, the tribunal will expect the complainant to have taken reasonable steps to find alternative employment.

Compensation may include compensation for loss of earnings, loss of job opportunity and/or for injury to feelings.

Damages for injury to feelings are awarded to compensate for the offence and distress caused by the act of discrimination. The amount awarded varies according to the particular circumstances of the case, and the degree of distress caused.

Compensation for loss of job opportunity is generally awarded where the complainant has failed to get a job because of discrimination. The size of the award will relate primarily to the disabled person's anticipated difficulty in obtaining similar employment, the rate of pay for the job in question, and how certain it is that he or she would have been appointed if not for discrimination.

An award for loss of earnings generally applies where a person has been dismissed, and is intended to compensate for financial loss caused by the dismissal.

An additional award of 'aggravated damages' may be made where the respondent has behaved in a high-handed, malicious, insulting or oppressive manner in committing the act of discrimination (*Alexander* v *The Home Office* [1988] IRLR 190, CA).

There is no financial limit on the amount of damages which may be awarded.

Regulations may require (subject to the tribunal's discretion) the payment of interest on compensation (s. 8(6)), as is the case with awards under the SDA 1975 and RRA 1976.

Declaration   Tribunals may make a declaration about the rights of the parties in relation to the matters to which the complaint relates. A declaration is purely a statement of the law (rather than a requirement that an employer take certain actions), and is likely to be appropriate in cases where the complainant has suffered no measurable loss, or where there is a point of principle involved.

Recommendation   Tribunals may recommend that the respondent take, within a specified period, 'reasonable' action to remove or reduce the adverse effect on the complainant of any matter to which the complaint relates (s. 8(2)(c)). (This differs slightly from the wording of the sex and race discrimination statutes, which requires the action to be 'practicable'.)

Recommendations under the RRA 1976 and SDA 1975 have mainly been made in cases involving practices of indirect discrimination. One tribunal, for example, recommended that a full-time teacher be allowed to return on a part-time basis after maternity leave, on a pro rata salary (*Hicks* v *North Yorkshire CC*, COIT 1643/117). Under the DDA 1995, a recommendation is likely to be appropriate, for example, where a tribunal decides that an employer is required to provide a suitable reasonable adjustment.

An Employment Appeal Tribunal case under the RRA 1975 held that a tribunal could not order an employer to appoint a successful complainant to the next available vacancy, because to promote a complainant without consideration of other applicants who might have better qualifications could amount to direct discrimination on the grounds of race (*British Gas* v *Sharma* [1991] IRLR 101, EAT). However, the same principle might not apply in DDA cases, because discrimination on the basis of disability is unlawful only if it is against a disabled person.

A recommendation can be made only where it relates to the circumstances of the individual complainant, and not to general discriminatory practices.

If the respondent fails to comply with such a recommendation without 'reasonable justification', the tribunal may order the payment of compensation or increase the amount of a compensation order already made (s. 8(5)). What will count as 'reasonable justification' will be a question of fact, varying from case to case.

Cost of litigation

Legal aid   Legal aid is not at present available to pay for representation before an industrial tribunal. However, there are proposals currently being considered by the Government to extend legal aid to tribunals, perhaps allowing particular 'franchised' legal advisers to be paid to provide representation.

Individuals can receive advice and help in preparing their case from solicitors paid for by the Legal Aid Board, provided that they fall within certain tight financial limits.

Costs of the other side   Generally speaking, an unsuccessful complainant will not have to pay the legal expenses (known as 'costs') of the successful party. A tribunal will order a complainant to pay the employer's costs only if he or she has acted 'frivolously' or 'vexaciously' in bringing or conducting the case, for example, a complainant who brings a claim knowing it to have no substance and no chance of success.

Appeals

A party to industrial tribunal proceedings can appeal only on certain narrow grounds:

(a)   that the tribunal has misdirected itself in law, or misunderstood or misapplied it;
(b)   that the tribunal misunderstood or misapplied the facts;
(c)   that the decision of the tribunal was perverse (i.e., that no tribunal, having applied the law correctly, could have reached that decision), or that there was no evidence to justify the conclusion. It is not enough to show that the tribunal relied on evidence which it was hard to believe.

Appeals are to the Employment Appeal Tribunal, and after that to the Court of Appeal. Legal aid may be available for such appeals (depending on whether a person meets the financial criteria, and is considered to have a strong enough case).

Goods and Services

A claim of unlawful discrimination in relation to goods and services must be brought by means of civil proceedings for tort in the county court in England and Wales, or in reparation for breach of a statutory duty in Scotland. Proceedings must be brought in the county court (or sheriff's court in Scotland) for the district in which the act of discrimination took place, or in which the discriminator's home or business is located.

If the only remedy being sought in proceedings is financial compensation, and the claim is for less than £3,000, then the claim must be brought in the small claims court. This is a division of the county court which operates with less formality and with simplified procedures. The major disadvantage is that legal aid is not available in the small claims court (see below).

Advice and assistance in enforcing the Part III provisions

There is scope within the 1995 Act for the Secretary of State to establish agencies to advise and promote the settlement of disputes (s. 28). At the time of passage of the law, the form that such assistance would take was unclear. The Government indicated that it intended to establish 'a network of advice points to provide advice and assistance to disabled people on the right of access to goods, facilities and services' (Lord Mackay, Hansard, 13 June 1995, 1697). No further details were provided, save that the network would be in place by the time that the Act came into force.

Time limit

Claims under Part III of the Act must be brought within six months of the incident of discrimination to which the claim relates (sch. 3, para. 6(1)). There are two exceptions. First, a court can consider a claim which has been made after the six-month limit if it considers that it is just and equitable to do so (sch. 3, para. 6(3)). Secondly, where the disabled person has consulted the network of assistance agencies established under s. 25 before the end of the six-month period, the time limit will be extended by a further two months (sch. 3, para. 6(2)).

Questionnaires

The questionnaire procedure available for claims of employment discrimination is not available for claims of discrimination in the provision of goods and services. County court procedures do, however, allow for a plaintiff to request further details about the reasons for a respondent's actions.

Proof

As with employment discrimination claims, the onus is on the plaintiff to establish on the balance of probabilities that an unlawful act of discrimination has been committed.

Remedies

The usual remedy where a claim for unlawful discrimination is established will be damages, including damages for injury to feelings. The DDA 1995 provides for a limit to be prescribed on the amount of damages which can be awarded as compensation for injury to feelings (sch. 3, para. 7). There are no comparable limits for damages for sex or race discrimination. It is envisaged that the limit will be set at the level at which cases are obliged to be brought in small claims courts.

A declaration or an injunction may also be granted. A declaration would purely involve a statement of the rights of the parties under the DDA, but would not require a provider of goods or services to take any action.

An injunction is an order requiring a party to do something, or to stop doing something. It will be appropriate, for example, where a disabled person has established his or her right to a reasonable adjustment. Unlike a recommendation in employment cases, if a provider of goods or services fails to comply with an injunction, the court may impose severe penalties (for example, committal to prison for contempt).

Cost of litigation

Legal aid Legal aid is not available for representation in proceedings brought in the small claims court. However, as with tribunal cases, a certain amount of advice and help in preparing a case from a solicitor may be paid for by the Legal Aid Board if the person comes within very tight financial limits.

If a case is brought in the county court, legal aid to pay for representation may be available if the party comes within the relevant financial limits (less stringent than for basic advice, but still quite restrictive) and the Legal Aid Board considers that the case is strong enough.

Costs of the other side The general rule in the county court is that the loser pays the winner's legal expenses. However, this rule does not apply in the small claims court, where each side pays its own expenses. Neither will it apply where the loser is receiving legal aid.

Appeal

A case can be appealed to the Court of Appeal, but only if the judge has misdirected himself on law, or if there was no evidence to support his finding of fact.

National Disability Council

The role of the National Disability Council (NDC) is to advise the Secretary of State on the operation of the Act and on the elimination of discrimination (s. 50(2)). It may, in the future, have additional functions conferred on it by the Secretary of State (s. 50(3)), but the Act does not permit such additional functions to include the investigation of any complaint which may be the subject of proceedings under the Act (s. 50(4)).

The NDC must prepare an annual report on its activities, to be placed before Parliament.

As well as conferring extremely limited powers on the NDC, the Act places certain additional restrictions on its ability to operate.

The NDC can only prepare a code of practice, providing guidance on specific aspects of the Act, at the request of the Secretary of State, and various requirements are established regarding consultation and Parliamentary approval (s. 52). The

Secretary of State may refuse to approve a draft code, in which case he must give the NDC a written reason for his refusal (s. 52(10)).

The NDC is unable (unless requested to do so by the Secretary of State) even to offer to advice on employment issues (s. 50(9)). The NACEPD, created in 1944, will continue to advise the Secretary of State in this field. This restriction will not apply if the Secretary of State utilises his power to abolish the NACEPD (s. 50(10)).

In addition, the NDC is required to have particular regard to the nature and extent of the benefits which would be likely to result from its recommendations, and to their likely cost, and is required to assess the likely financial benefits and cost of implementing its recommendations (s. 50(5) and (6)).

Prior to advising the Secretary of State, the NDC must consult, and have regard to the response of, such persons as it considers appropriate, and in particular must consult any other statutory bodies which provide advice in relation to disability and have functions relevant to the particular issue (s. 50(7)).

The NDC will have at least ten, and not more than 20, members, to be appointed by the Secretary of State (sch. 5, paras 3(1) and (3)). Members must either have knowledge or experience of the needs of disabled people (or a particular group of disabled persons) or people who have been disabled, or be members of professional bodies or bodies which represent industry or other business interests (sch. 5, para. 5). The Secretary of State is required to try to ensure that at least half the members of the Council are disabled persons, persons who have had a disability, or the parents or guardians of disabled people (sch. 5, para. 7).

Northern Ireland

A separate Northern Ireland Disability Council is established with equivalent powers and duties to the National Disability Council (sch. 8).

Disability Discrimination Act 1995

CHAPTER 50

ARRANGEMENT OF SECTIONS

PART I   DISABILITY

PART II   EMPLOYMENT

Discrimination by employers

Enforcement etc.

Discrimination by other persons

Premises occupied under leases

PART VI   THE NATIONAL DISABILITY COUNCIL

PART VII   SUPPLEMENTAL

PART VIII   MISCELLANEOUS

SCHEDULES:

Disability Discrimination Act 1995

An Act to make it unlawful to discriminate against disabled persons in connection with employment, the provision of goods, facilities and services or the disposal or management of premises; to make provision about the employment of disabled persons; and to establish a National Disability Council.   [8th November 1995]

BE IT ENACTED by the Queen's most Excellent Majesty, by and with the advice and consent of the Lords Spiritual and Temporal, and Commons, in this present Parliament assembled, and by the authority of the same, as follows:—

PART I   DISABILITY

1.   Meaning of 'disability' and 'disabled person'
(1)   Subject to the provisions of Schedule 1, a person has a disability for the purposes of this Act if he has a physical or mental impairment which has a substantial and long-term adverse effect on his ability to carry out normal day-to-day activities.

(2)   In this Act 'disabled person' means a person who has a disability.

2.   Past disabilities
(1)   The provisions of this Part and Parts II and III apply in relation to a person who has had a disability as they apply in relation to a person who has that disability.

(2)   Those provisions are subject to the modifications made by Schedule 2.

(3)   Any regulations or order made under this Act may include provision with respect to persons who have had a disability.

(4)   In any proceedings under Part II or Part III of this Act, the question whether a person had a disability at a particular time ('the relevant time') shall be determined, for the purposes of this section, as if the provisions of, or made under, this Act in force when the act complained of was done had been in force at the relevant time.

(5)   The relevant time may be a time before the passing of this Act.

3.   Guidance
(1)   The Secretary of State may issue guidance about the matters to be taken into account in determining—

   (a)   whether an impairment has a substantial adverse effect on a person's ability to carry out normal day-to-day activities; or

   (b)   whether such an impairment has a long-term effect.

(2)   The guidance may, among other things, give examples of—

(a)   effects which it would be reasonable, in relation to particular activities, to regard for purposes of this Act as substantial adverse effects;

(b)   effects which it would not be reasonable, in relation to particular activities, to regard for such purposes as substantial adverse effects;

(c)   substantial adverse effects which it would be reasonable to regard, for such purposes, as long-term;

(d)   substantial adverse effects which it would not be reasonable to regard, for such purposes, as long-term.

(3)   A tribunal or court determining, for any purpose of this Act, whether an impairment has a substantial and long-term adverse effect on a person's ability to carry out normal day-to-day activities, shall take into account any guidance which appears to it to be relevant.

(4)   In preparing a draft of any guidance, the Secretary of State shall consult such persons as he considers appropriate.

(5)   Where the Secretary of State proposes to issue any guidance, he shall publish a draft of it, consider any representations that are made to him about the draft and, if he thinks it appropriate, modify his proposals in the light of any of those representations.

(6)   If the Secretary of State decides to proceed with any proposed guidance, he shall lay a draft of it before each House of Parliament.

(7)   If, within the 40-day period, either House resolves not to approve the draft, the Secretary of State shall take no further steps in relation to the proposed guidance.

(8)   If no such resolution is made within the 40-day period, the Secretary of State shall issue the guidance in the form of his draft.

(9)   The guidance shall come into force on such date as the Secretary of State may appoint by order.

(10)   Subsection (7) does not prevent a new draft of the proposed guidance from being laid before Parliament.

(11)   The Secretary of State may—

(a)   from time to time revise the whole or part of any guidance and re-issue it;

(b)   by order revoke any guidance.

(12)   In this section—

'40-day period', in relation to the draft of any proposed guidance, means—

(a)   if the draft is laid before one House on a day later than the day on which it is laid before the other House, the period of 40 days beginning with the later of the two days, and

(b)   in any other case, the period of 40 days beginning with the day on which the draft is laid before each House,

no account being taken of any period during which Parliament is dissolved or prorogued or during which both Houses are adjourned for more than 4 days; and

'guidance' means guidance issued by the Secretary of State under this section and includes guidance which has been revised and re-issued.

PART II   EMPLOYMENT

Discrimination by employers

4.   Discrimination against applicants and employees

(1)   It is unlawful for an employer to discriminate against a disabled person—

(a)   in the arrangements which he makes for the purpose of determining to whom he should offer employment;

(b)   In the terms on which he offers that person employment; or

(c)   by refusing to offer, or deliberately not offering, him employment.

(2)   It is unlawful for an employer to discriminate against a disabled person whom he employs—

(a)   in the terms of employment which he affords him;

(b)   in the opportunities which he affords him for promotion, a transfer, training or receiving any other benefit;

(c)   by refusing to afford him, or deliberately not affording him, any such opportunity; or

(d)   by dismissing him, or subjecting him to any other detriment.

(3)   Subsection (2) does not apply to benefits of any description if the employer is concerned with the provision (whether or not for payment) of benefits of that description to the public, or to a section of the public which includes the employee in question, unless—

(a)   that provision differs in a material respect from the provision of the benefits by the employer to his employees; or

(b)   the provision of the benefits to the employee in question is regulated by his contract of employment; or

(c)   the benefits relate to training.

(4)   In this Part 'benefits' includes facilities and services.

(5)   In the case of an act which constitutes discrimination by virtue of section 55, this section also applies to discrimination against a person who is not disabled.

(6)   This section applies only in relation to employment at an establishment in Great Britain.

5.   Meaning of 'discrimination'

(1)   For the purposes of this Part, an employer discriminates against a disabled person if—

(a)   for a reason which relates to the disabled person's disability, he treats him less favourably than he treats or would treat others to whom that reason does not or would not apply; and

(b)   he cannot show that the treatment in question is justified.

(2)   For the purposes of this Part, an employer also discriminates against a disabled person if—

(a)   he fails to comply with a section 6 duty imposed on him in relation to the disabled person; and

(b)   he cannot show that his failure to comply with that duty is justified.

(3)   Subject to subsection (5), for the purposes of subsection (1) treatment is justified if, but only if, the reason for it is both material to the circumstances of the particular case and substantial.

(4)   For the purposes of subsection (2), failure to comply with a section 6 duty is justified if, but only if, the reason for the failure is both material to the circumstances of the particular case and substantial.

(5)   If, in a case falling within subsection (1), the employer is under a section 6 duty in relation to the disabled person but fails without justification to comply with

that duty, his treatment of that person cannot be justified under subsection (3) unless it would have been justified even if he had complied with the section 6 duty.

(6) Regulations may make provision, for purposes of this section, as to circumstances in which—

    (a)   treatment is to be taken to be justified;

    (b)   failure to comply with a section 6 duty is to be taken to be justified;

    (c)   treatment is to be taken not to be justified;

    (d)   failure to comply with a section 6 duty is to be taken not to be justified.

(7) Regulations under subsection (6) may, in particular—

    (a)   make provision by reference to the cost of affording any benefit; and

    (b)   in relation to benefits under occupational pension schemes, make provision with a view to enabling uniform rates of contributions to be maintained.

6. Duty of employer to make adjustments

(1) Where—

    (a)   any arrangements made by or on behalf of an employer, or

    (b)   any physical feature of premises occupied by the employer,

place the disabled person concerned at a substantial disadvantage in comparison with persons who are not disabled, it is the duty of the employer to take such steps as it is reasonable, in all the circumstances of the case, for him to have to take in order to prevent the arrangements or feature having that effect.

(2) Subsection (1)(a) applies only in relation to—

    (a)   arrangements for determining to whom employment should be offered;

    (b)   any term, condition or arrangements on which employment, promotion, a transfer, training or any other benefit is offered or afforded.

(3) The following are examples of steps which an employer may have to take in relation to a disabled person in order to comply with subsection (1)—

    (a)   making adjustments to premises;

    (b)   allocating some of the disabled person's duties to another person;

    (c)   transferring him to fill an existing vacancy;

    (d)   altering his working hours;

    (e)   assigning him to a different place of work;

    (f)   allowing him to be absent during working hours for rehabilitation, assessment or treatment;

    (g)   giving him, or arranging for him to be given, training;

    (h)   acquiring or modifying equipment;

    (i)   modifying instructions or reference manuals;

    (j)   modifying procedures for testing or assessment;

    (k)   providing a reader or interpreter;

    (l)   providing supervision.

(4) In determining whether it is reasonable for an employer to have to take a particular step in order to comply with subsection (1), regard shall be had, in particular, to—

    (a)   the extent to which taking the step would prevent the effect in question;

    (b)   the extent to which it is practicable for the employer to take the step;

    (c)   the financial and other costs which would be incurred by the employer in taking the step and the extent to which taking it would disrupt any of his activities;

    (d)   the extent of the employer's financial and other resources;

(e)   the availability to the employer of financial or other assistance with respect to taking the step.

This subsection is subject to any provision of regulations made under subsection (8).

(5)   In this section, 'the disabled person concerned' means—

(a)   in the case of arrangements for determining to whom employment should be offered, any disabled person who is, or has notified the employer that he may be, an applicant for that employment;

(b)   in any other case, a disabled person who is—

(i)   an applicant for the employment concerned; or

(ii)   an employee of the employer concerned.

(6)   Nothing in this section imposes any duty on an employer in relation to a disabled person if the employer does not know, and could not reasonably be expected to know—

(a)   in the case of an applicant or potential applicant, that the disabled person concerned is, or may be, an applicant for the employment; or

(b)   in any case, that that person has a disability and is likely to be affected in the way mentioned in subsection (1).

(7)   Subject to the provisions of this section, nothing in this Part is to be taken to require an employer to treat a disabled person more favourably than he treats or would treat others.

(8)   Regulations may make provision, for the purposes of subsection (1)—

(a)   as to circumstances in which arrangements are, or a physical feature is, to be taken to have the effect mentioned in that subsection;

(b)   as to circumstances in which arrangements are not, or a physical feature is not, to be taken to have that effect;

(c)   as to circumstances in which it is reasonable for an employer to have to take steps of a prescribed description;

(d)   as to steps which it is always reasonable for an employer to have to take;

(e)   as to circumstances in which it is not reasonable for an employer to have to take steps of a prescribed description;

(f)   as to steps which it is never reasonable for an employer to have to take;

(g)   as to things which are to be treated as physical features;

(h)   as to things which are not to be treated as such features.

(9)   Regulations made under subsection (8)(c), (d), (e) or (f) may, in particular, make provision by reference to the cost of taking the steps concerned.

(10)   Regulations may make provision adding to the duty imposed on employers by this section, including provision of a kind which may be made under subsection (8).

(11)   This section does not apply in relation to any benefit under an occupational pension scheme or any other benefit payable in money or money's worth under a scheme or arrangement for the benefit of employees in respect of—

(a)   termination of service;

(b)   retirement, old age or death;

(c)   accident, injury, sickness or invalidity; or

(d)   any other prescribed matter.

(12)   This section imposes duties only for the purpose of determining whether an employer has discriminated against a disabled person; and accordingly a breach of any such duty is not actionable as such.

7. Exemption for small businesses

(1) Nothing in this Part applies in relation to an employer who has fewer than 20 employees.

(2) The Secretary of State may by order amend subsection (1) by substituting a different number (not greater than 20) for the number for the time being specified there.

(3) In this section—

'anniversary' means the anniversary of the coming into force of this section; and

'review' means a review of the effect of this section.

(4) Before making any order under subsection (2), the Secretary of State shall conduct a review.

(5) Unless he has already begun or completed a review under subsection (4), the Secretary of State shall begin to conduct a review immediately after the fourth anniversary.

(6) Any review shall be completed within nine months.

(7) In conducting any review, the Secretary of State shall consult—

(a) such organisations representing the interests of employers as he considers appropriate; any

(b) such organisations representing the interests of disabled persons in employment or seeking employment as he considers appropriate.

(8) If, on completing a review, the Secretary of State decides to make an order under subsection (2), he shall make such an order to come into force not later than one year after the commencement of the review.

(9) If, on completing a review, the Secretary of State decides not to make such an order, he shall not later than one year after the commencement of the review lay before Parliament a report—

(a) summarising the results of the review; and

(b) giving the reasons for his decision.

(10) Any report made by the Secretary of State under subsection (9) shall include a summary of the views expressed to him in his consultations.

Enforcement etc.

8. Enforcement, remedies and procedure

(1) A complaint by any person that another person—

(a) has discriminated against him in a way which is unlawful under this Part, or

(b) is, by virtue of section 57 or 58, to be treated as having discriminated against him in such a way,

may be presented to an industrial tribunal.

(2) Where an industrial tribunal finds that a complaint presented to it under this section is well-founded, it shall take such of the following steps as it considers just and equitable—

(a) making a declaration as to the rights of the complainant and the respondent in relation to the matters to whch the complaint relates;

(b) ordering the respondent to pay compensation to the complainant;

(c) recommending that the respondent take, within a specified period, action appearing to the tribunal to be reasonable, in all the circumstances of the case, for the purpose of obviating or reducing the adverse effect on the complainant of any matter to which the complaint relates.

(3)   Where a tribunal orders compensation under subsection (2)(b), the amount of the compensation shall be calculated by applying the principles applicable to the calculation of damages in claims in tort or (in Scotland) in reparation for breach of statutory duty.

(4)   For the avoidance of doubt it is hereby declared that compensation in respect of discrimination in a way which is unlawful under this Part may include compensation for injury to feelings whether or not it includes compensation under any other head.

(5)   If the respondent to a complaint fails, without reasonable justification, to comply with a recommendation made by an industrial tribunal under subsection (2)(c) the tribunal may, if it thinks it just and equitable to do so—

(a)   increase the amount of compensation required to be paid to the complainant in respect of the complaint, where an order was made under subsection (2)(b); or

(b)   make an order under subsection (2)(b).

(6)   Regulations may make provision—

(a)   for enabling a tribunal, where an amount of compensation falls to be awarded under subsection (2)(b), to include in the award interest on that amount; and

(b)   specifying, for cases where a tribunal decides that an award is to include an amount in respect of interest, the manner in which and the periods and rate by reference to which the interest is to be determined.

(7)   Regulations may modify the operation of any order made under paragraph 6A of Schedule 9 to the Employment Protection (Consolidation) Act 1978 (power to make provision as to interest on sums payable in pursuance of industrial tribunal decisions) to the extent that it relates to an award of compensation under subsection (2)(b).

(8)   Part I of Schedule 3 makes further provision about the enforcement of this Part and about procedure.

9.   Validity of certain agreements

(1)   Any term in a contract of employment or other agreement is void so far as it purports to—

(a)   require a person to do anything which would contravene any provision of, or made under, this Part;

(b)   exclude or limit the operation of any provision of this Part; or

(c)   prevent any person from presenting a complaint to an industrial tribunal under this Part.

(2)   Paragraphs (b) and (c) of subsection (1) do not apply to an agreement not to institute proceedings under section 8(1), or to an agreement not to continue such proceedings, if—

(a)   a conciliation officer has acted under paragraph 1 of Schedule 3 in relation to the matter; or

(b)   the conditions set out in subsection (3) are satisfied.

(3)   The conditions are that—

(a)   the complainant must have received independent legal advice from a qualified lawyer as to the terms and effect of the proposed agreement (and in particular its effect on his ability to pursue his complaint before an industrial tribunal);

(b)   when the adviser gave the advice there must have been in force a policy of insurance covering the risk of a claim by the complainant in respect of loss arising in consequence of the advice; and

(c)   the agreement must be in writing, relate to the particular complaint, identify the adviser and state that the conditions are satisfied.

(4)   In this section—

'independent', in relation to legal advice to the complainant, means that it is given by a lawyer who is not acting for the other party or for a person who is connected with that other party; and

'qualified lawyer' means—

(a)   as respects proceedings in England and Wales, a barrister (whether in practice as such or employed to give legal advice) or a solicitor of the Supreme Court who holds a practising certificate; and

(b)   as respects proceedings in Scotland, an advocate (whether in practice as such or employed to give legal advice) or a solicitor who holds a practising certificate.

(5)   For the purposes of subsection (4), any two persons are to be treated as connected if—

(a)   one is a company of which the other (directly or indirectly) has control, or

(b)   both are companies of which a third person (directly or indirectly) has control.

10.   Charities and support for particular groups of persons

(1)   Nothing in this Part—

(a)   affects any charitable instrument which provides for conferring benefits on one or more categories of person determined by reference to any physical or mental capacity; or

(b)   makes unlawful any act done by a charity or recognised body in pursuance of any of its charitable purposes, so far as those purposes are connected with persons so determined.

(2)   Nothing in this Part prevents—

(a)   a person who provides supported employment from treating members of a particular group of disabled persons more favourably than other persons in providing such employment; or

(b)   the Secretary of State from agreeing to arrangements for the provision of supported employment which will, or may, have that effect.

(3)   In this section—

'charitable instrument' means an enactment or other instrument (whenever taking effect) so far as it relates to charitable purposes;

'charity' has the same meaning as in the Charities Act 1993;

'recognised body' means a body which is a recognised body for the purposes of Part I of the Law Reform (Miscellaneous Provisions) (Scotland) Act 1990; and

'supported employment' means facilities provided, or in respect of which payments are made, under section 15 of the Disabled Persons (Employment) Act 1944.

(4)   In the application of this section to England and Wales, 'charitable purposes' means purposes which are exclusively charitable according to the law of England and Wales.

(5)   In this application of this section to Scotland, 'charitable purposes' shall be construed in the same way as if it were contained in the Income Tax Acts.

11.   Advertisements suggesting that employers will discriminate against disabled persons

(1)   This section applies where—

(a)   a disabled person has applied for employment with an employer;

(b)   the employer has refused to offer, or has deliberately not offered, him the employment;

(c)   the disabled person has presented a complaint under section 8 against the employer;

(d)   the employer has advertised the employment (whether before or after the disabled person applied for it); and

(e)   the advertisement indicated, or might reasonably be understood to have indicated, that any application for the advertised employment would, or might, be determined to any extent by reference to—

(i)   the successful applicant not having any disability or any category of disability which includes the disabled person's disability; or

(ii)   the employer's reluctance to take any action of a kind mentioned in section 6.

(2)   The tribunal hearing the complaint shall assume, unless the contrary is shown, that the employer's reason for refusing to offer, or deliberately not offering, the employment to the complainant as related to the complainant's disability.

(3)   In this section 'advertisement' includes every form of advertisement or notice, whether to the public or not.

Discrimination by other persons

12.   Discrimination against contract workers

(1)   It is unlawful for a principal, in relation to contract work, to discriminate against a disabled person—

(a)   in the terms on which he allows him to do that work;

(b)   by not allowing him to do it or continue to do it;

(c)   in the way he affords him access to any benefits or by refusing or deliberately omitting to afford him access to them; or

(d)   by subjecting him to any other detriment.

(2)   Subsection (1) does not apply to benefits of any description if the principal is concerned with the provision (whether or not for payment) of benefits of that description to the public, or to a section of the public which includes the contract worker in question, unless that provision differs in a material respect from the provision of the benefits by the principal to contract workers.

(3)   The provisions of this Part (other than subsections (1) to (3) of section 4) apply to any principal, in relation to contract work, as if he were, or would be, the employer of the contract worker supplied to do work for him were an employee of his.

(4)   In the case of an act which constitutes discrimination by virtue of section 55, this section also applies to discrimination against a person who is not disabled.

(5)   This section applies only in relation to contract work done at an establishment in Great Britain (the provisions of section 68 about the meaning of 'employment at an establishment in Great Britain' applying for the purposes of this subsection with the appropriate modifications).

(6)   In this section—

'principal' means a person ('A') who makes work available for doing by individuals who are employed by another person who supplies them under a contract made with A;

'contract work' means work so made available; and

'contract worker' means any individual who is supplied to the principal under such a contract.

13.   Discrimination by trade organisations

(1)   It is unlawful for a trade organisation to discriminate against a disabled person—

(a)   in the terms on which it is prepared to admit him to membership of the organisation; or

(b)   by refusing to accept, or deliberately not accepting, his application for membership.

(2)   It is unlawful for a trade organisation, in the case of a disabled person who is a member of the organisation, to discriminate against him—

(a)   in the way it affords him access to any benefits or by refusing or deliberately omitting to afford him access to them;

(b)   by depriving him of membership, or varying the terms on which he is a member; or

(c)   by subjecting him to any other detriment.

(3)   In this case of an act which constitutes discrimination by virtue of section 55, this section also applies to discrimination against a person who is not disabled.

(4)   In this section 'trade organisation' means an organisation of workers, an organisation of employers or any other organisation whose members carry on a particular profession or trade for the purposes of which the organisation exists.

14.   Meaning of 'discrimination' in relation to trade organisations

(1)   For the purposes of this Part, a trade organisation discriminates against a disabled person if—

(a)   for a reason which relates to the disabled person's disability, it treats him less favourably than it treats or would treat others to whom that reason does not or would not apply; and

(b)   it cannot show that the treatment in question is justified.

(2)   For the purposes of this Part, a trade organisation also discriminates against a disabled person if—

(a)   it fails to comply with a section 15 duty imposed on it in relation to the disabled person; and

(b)   it cannot show that its failure to comply with that duty is justified.

(3)   Subject to subsection (5), for the purposes of subsection (1) treatment is justified if, but only if, the reason for it is both material to the circumstances of the particular case and substantial.

(4)   For the purposes of subsection (2), failure to comply with a section 15 duty is justified if, but only if, the reason for the failure is both material to the circumstances of the particular case and substantial.

(5)   If, in a case falling within subsection (1), the trade organisation is under a section 15 duty in relation to the disabled person concerned but fails without justification to comply with that duty, its treatment of that person cannot be justified under subsection (3) unless the treatment would have been justified even if the organisation had complied with the section 15 duty.

(6)   Regulations may make provision, for purposes of this section, as to circumstances in which—
    (a)   treatment is to be taken to be justified;
    (b)   failure to comply with a section 15 duty is to be taken not to be justified.
    (c)   treatment is to be taken not to be justified;
    (d)   failure to comply with a section 15 duty is to be taken not to be justified.

15.   [Duty of trade organisation to make adjustments]

(1)   Where—
    (a)   any arrangements made by or on behalf of a trade organisation, or
    (b)   any physical feature of premises occupied by the organisation,
place the disabled person concerned at a substantial disadvantage in comparison with persons who are not disabled, it is the duty of the organisation to take such steps as it is reasonable, in all the circumstances of the case, for it to have to take in order to prevent the arrangements or feature having that effect.

(2)   Subsection (1)(a) applies only in relation to—
    (a)   arrangements for determining who should become or remain a member of the organisation;
    (b)   any term, condition or arrangements on which membership or any benefit is offered or afforded.

(3)   In determining whether it is reasonable for a trade organisation to have to take a particular step in order to comply with subsection (1), regard shall be had, in particular, to—
    (a)   the extent to which taking the step would prevent the effect in question;
    (b)   the extent to which it is practicable for the organisation to take the step;
    (c)   the financial and other costs which would be incurred by the organisation in taking the step and the extent to which taking it would disrupt any of its activities;
    (d)   the extent of the organisation's financial and other resources;
    (e)   the availability to the organisation of financial or other assistance with respect to taking the step.
This subsection is subject to any provision of regulations made under subsection (7).

(4)   In this section 'the disabled person concerned' means—
    (a)   in the case of arrangements for determining to whom membership should be offered, any disabled person who is, or has notified the organisation that he may be, an applicant for membership;
    (b)   in any other case, a disabled person who is—
        (i)   an application for membership; or
        (ii)   a member of the organisation.

(5)   Nothing in this section imposes any duty on an organisation in relation to a disabled person if the organisation does not know, and could not reasonably be expected to know that the disabled person concerned—
    (a)   is, or may be, an applicant for membership; or

(b) has a disability and is likely to be affected in the way mentioned in subsection (1).

(6) Subject to the provisions of this section, nothing in this Part is to be taken to require a trade organisation to treat a disabled person more favourably than it treats or would treat others.

(7) Regulations may make provision for the purposes of subsection (1) as to any of the matters mentioned in paragraphs (a) to (h) of section 6(8) (the references in those paragraphs to an employer being read for these purposes as references to a trade organisation).

(8) Subsection (9) of section 6 applies in relation to such regulations as it applies in relation to regulations made under section 6(8).

(9) Regulations may make provision adding to the duty imposed on trade organisations by this section, including provision of a kind which may be made under subsection (7).

(10) This section imposes duties only for the purpose of determining whether a trade organisation has discriminated against a disabled person; and accordingly a breach of any such duty is not actionable as such.

Premises occupied under leases

16. Alterations to premises occupied under leases

(1) This section applies where—

(a) an employer or trade organisation ('the occupier') occupies premises under a lease;

(b) but for this section, the occupier would not be entitled to make a particular alteration to the premises; and

(c) the alteration is one which the occupier proposes to make in order to comply with a section 6 duty or section 15 duty.

(2) Except to the extent to which it expressly so provides, the lease shall have effect by virtue of this subsection as if it provided—

(a) for the occupier to be entitled to make the alteration with the written consent of the lessor;

(b) for the occupier to have to make a written application to the lessor for consent if he wishes to make the alteration;

(c) if such an application is made, for the lessor not to withhold his consent unreasonably; and

(d) for the lessor to be entitled to make his consent subject to reasonable conditions.

(3) In this section—

'lease' includes a tenancy, sub-lease or sub-tenancy and an agreement for a lease, tenancy, sub-lease or sub-tenancy; and

'sub-lease' and 'sub-tenancy' have such meaning as may be prescribed.

(4) If the terms and conditions of a lease—

(a) impose conditions which are to apply if the occupier alters the premises, or

(b) entitle the lessor to impose conditions when consenting to the occupier's altering the premises,

the occupier is to be treated for the purposes of subsection (1) as not being entitled to make the alteration.

(5) Part I of Schedule 4 supplements the provisions of this section.

Occupational pension schemes and insurance services

17. Occupational pension schemes

(1)   Every occupational pension scheme shall be taken to include a provision ('a non-discrimination rule')—

    (a)   relating to the terms on which—

        (i)   persons become members of the scheme; and

        (ii)   members of the scheme are treated; and

    (b)   requiring the trustees or managers of the scheme to refrain from any act or omission which, if done in relation to a person by an employer, would amount to unlawful discrimination against that person for the purposes of this Part.

(2)   The other provisions of the scheme are to have effect subject to the non-discrimination rule.

(3)   Without prejudice to section 67, regulations under this Part may—

    (a)   with respect to trustees or managers of occupational pension schemes make different provision from that made with respect to employers; or

    (b)   make provision modifying the application to such trustees or managers of any regulations made under this Part, or of any provisions of this Part so far as they apply to employers.

(4)   In determining, for the purposes of this section, whether an act or omission would amount to unlawful discrimination if done by an employer, any provision made under subsection (3) shall be applied as if it applied in relation to the notional employer.

18. Insurance services

(1)   This section applies where a provider of insurance services ('the insurer') enters into arrangements with an employer under which the employer's employees, or a class of his employees—

    (a)   receive insurance services provided by the insurer; or

    (b)   are given an opportunity to receive such services.

(2)   The insurer is to be taken, for the purposes of this Part, to discriminate unlawfully against a disabled person who is a relevant employee if he acts in relation to that employee in a way which would be unlawful discrimination for the purposes of Part III if—

    (a)   he were providing the service in question to members of the public; and

    (b)   the employee was provided with, or was trying to secure the provision of, that service as a member of the public.

(3)   In this section—

'insurance services' means services of a prescribed description for the provision of benefits in respect of—

    (a)   termination of service;

    (b)   retirement, old age or death;

    (c)   accident, injury, sickness or invalidity; or

    (d)   any other prescribed matter; and

'relevant employee' means—

    (a)   in the case of an arrangement which applies to employees of the employer in question, an employee of his;

    (b)   in the case of an arrangement which applies to a class of employees of the employer, an employee who is in that class.

(4) For the purposes of the definition of 'relevant employee' in subsection (3), 'employee', in relation to an employer, includes a person who has applied for, or is contemplating applying for, employment by that employer or (as the case may be) employment by him in the class in question.

PART III   DISCRIMINATION IN OTHER AREAS

Goods, facilities and services

19.   Discrimination in relation to goods, facilities and services

(1) It is unlawful for a provider of services to discriminte against a disabled person—

(a) in refusing to provide, or deliberately not providing, to the disabled person any service which he provides, or is prepared to provide, to members of the public;

(b) in failing to comply with any duty imposed on him by section 21 in circumstances in which the effect of that failure is to make it impossible or unreasonably difficult for the disabled person to make use of any such service;

(c) in the standard of service which he provides to the disabled person or the manner in which he provides it to him; or

(d) in the terms on which he provides a service to the disabled person.

(2) For the purposes of this section and sections 20 and 21—

(a) the provision of services includes the provision of any goods or facilities;

(b) a person is 'a provider of services' if he is concerned with the provision, in the United Kingdom, of services to the public or to a section of the public; and

(c) it is irrelevant whether a service is provided on payment or without payment.

(3) The following are examples of services to which this section and sections 20 and 21 apply—

(a) access to and use of any place which members of the public are permitted to enter;

(b) access to and use of means of communication;

(c) access to and use of information services;

(d) accommodation in a hotel, boarding house or other similar establishment;

(e) facilities by way of banking or insurance or for grants, loans, credit or finance;

(f) facilities for entertainment, recreation or refreshment;

(g) facilities provided by employment agencies or under section 2 of the Employment and Training Act 1973;

(h) the services of any profession or trade, or any local or other public authority.

(4) In the case of an act which constitutes discrimination by virtue of section 55, this section also applies to discrimination against a person who is not disabled.

(5) Except in such circumstances as may be prescribed, this section and sections 20 and 21 do not apply to—

(a) education which is funded, or secured, by a relevant body or provided at—

(i) an establishment which is funded by such a body or by a Minister of the Crown; or

(ii)   any other establishment which is a school as defined in section 14(5) of the Further and Higher Education Act 1992 or section 135(1) of the Education (Scotland) Act 1980;
  (b)   any service so far as it consists of the use of any means of transport; or
  (c)   such other services as may be prescribed.
  (6)   In subsection (5) 'relevant body' means—
  (a)   a local education authority in England and Wales;
  (b)   an education authority in Scotland;
  (c)   the Funding Agency for Schools;
  (d)   the Schools Funding Council for Wales;
  (e)   the Further Education Funding Council for England;
  (f)   the Further Education Funding Coucil for Wales;
  (g)   the Higher Education Funding Council for England;
  (h)   the Scottish Higher Education Funding Council;
  (i)   the Higher Education Funding Council for Wales;
  (j)   the Teacher Training Agency;
  (k)   a voluntary organisation; or
  (l)   a body of a prescribed kind.

20.   Meaning of 'discrimination'

  (1)   For the purposes of section 19, a provider of services discriminates against a disabled person if—
  (a)   for a reason which relates to the disabled person's disability, he treats him less favourably than he treats or would treat others to whom that reason does not or would not apply; and
  (b)   he cannot show that the treatment in question is justified.
  (2)   For the purposes of section 19, a provider of services also discriminates against a disabled person if—
  (a)   he fails to comply with a section 21 duty imposed on him in relation to the disabled person; and
  (b)   he cannot show that his failure to comply with that duty is justified.
  (3)   For the purposes of this section, treatment is justified only if—
  (a)   in the opinion of the provider of services, one or more of the conditions mentioned in subsection (4) are satisfied; and
  (b)   it is reasonable, in all the circumstances of the case, for him to hold that opinion.
  (4)   The conditions are that—
  (a)   in any case, the treatment is necessary in order not to endanger the health or safety of any person (which may include that of the disabled person);
  (b)   in any case, the disabled person is incapable of entering into an enforceable agreement, or of giving an informed consent, and for that reason the treatment is reasonable in that case;
  (c)   in a case falling within section 19(1)(a), the treatment is necessary because the provider of services would otherwise be unable to provide the service to members of the public;
  (d)   in a case falling within section 19(1)(c) or (d), the treatment is necessary in order for the provider of services to be able to provide the service to the disabled person or to other members of the public;

(e)   in a case falling within section 19(1)(d), the difference in the terms on which the service is provided to the disabled person and those on which it is provided to other members of the public reflects the greater cost to the provider of services in providing the service to the disabled person.

(5)   Any increase in the cost of providing a service to a disabled person which results from compliance by a provider of services with a section 21 duty shall be disregarded for the purposes of subsection (4)(e).

(6)   Regulations may make provision, for purposes of this section, as to circumstances in which—

(a)   it is reasonable for a provider of services to hold the opinion mentioned in subsection (3)(a);

(b)   it is not reasonable for a provider of services to hold that opinion.

(7)   Regulations may make provision for subsection (4)(b) not to apply in prescribed circumstances where—

(a)   a person is acting for a disabled person under a power of attorney;

(b)   functions conferred by or under Part VII of the Mental Health Act 1983 are exercisable in relation to a disabled person's property or affairs; or

(c)   powers are exercisable in Scotland in relation to a disabled person's property or affairs in consequence of the appointment of a curator bonis, tutor or judicial factor.

(8)   Regulations may make provision, for purposes of this section, as to circumstances (other than those mentioned in subsection (4)) in which treatment is to be taken to be justified.

(9)   In subsections (3), (4) and (8) 'treatment' includes failure to comply with a section 21 duty.

21.   Duty of providers of services to make adjustments

(1)   Where a provider of services has a practice, policy or procedure which makes it impossible or unreasonably difficult for disabled persons to make use of a service which he provides, or is prepared to provide, to other members of the public, it is his duty to take such steps as it is reasonable, in all the circumstances of the case, for him to have to take in order to change that practice, policy or procedure so that it no longer has that effect.

(2)   Where a physical feature (for example, one arising from the design or construction of a building or the approach or access to premises) makes it impossible or unreasonably difficult for disabled persons to make use of such a service, it is the duty of the provider of that service to take such steps as it is reasonable, in all the circumstances of the case, for him to have to take in order to—

(a)   remove the feature;

(b)   alter it so that it no longer has that effect;

(c)   provide a reasonable means of avoiding the feature; or

(d)   provide a reasonable alternative method of making the service in question available to disabled persons.

(3)   Regulations may prescribe—

(a)   matters which are to be taken into account in determining whether any provision of a kind mentioned in subsection (2)(c) or (d) is reasonable; and

(b)   categories of providers of services to whom subsection (2) does not apply.

(4)   Where an auxiliary aid or service (for example, the provision of information on audio tape or of a sign language interpreter) would—

(a)   enable disabled persons to make use of a service which a provider of services provides, or is prepared to provide, to members of the public, or

(b)   facilitate the use by disabled persons of such a service,

it is the duty of the provider of that service to take such steps as it is reasonable, in all the circumstances of the case, for him to have to take in order to provide that auxiliary aid or service.

(5)   Regulations may make provision, for the purposes of this section—

(a)   as to circumstances in which it is reasonable for a provider of services to have to take steps of a prescribed description;

(b)   as to circumstances in which it is not reasonable for a provider of services to have to take steps of a prescribed description;

(c)   as to what is to be included within the meaning of 'practice, policy or procedure';

(d)   as to what is not to be included within the meaning of that expression;

(e)   as to things which are to be treated as physical features;

(f)   as to things which are not to be treated as such features;

(g)   as to things which are to be treated as auxiliary aids or services;

(h)   as to things which are not to be treated as auxiliary aids or services.

(6)   Nothing in this section requires a provider of services to take any steps which would fundamentally alter the nature of the service in question or the nature of his trade, profession or business.

(7)   Nothing in this section requires a provider of services to take any steps which would cause him to incur expenditure exceeding the prescribed maximum.

(8)   Regulations under subsection (7) may provide for the prescribed maximum to be calculated by reference to—

(a)   aggregate amounts of expenditure incurred in relation to different cases;

(b)   prescribed periods;

(c)   services of a prescribed description;

(d)   premises of a prescribed description; or

(e)   such other criteria as may be prescribed.

(9)   Regulations may provide, for the purposes of subsection (7), for expenditure incurred by one provider of services to be treated as incurred by another.

(10)   This section imposes duties only for the purpose of determining whether a provider of services has discriminated against a disabled person; and accordingly a breach of any such duty is not actionable as such.

Premises

22.   Discrimination in relation to premises

(1)   It is unlawful for a person with power to dispose of any premises to discriminate against a disabled person—

(a)   in the terms on which he offers to dispose of those premises to the disabled person;

(b)   by refusing to dispose of those premises to the disabled person; or

(c)   in his treatment of the disabled person in relation to any list of persons in need of premises of that description.

(2)   Subsection (1) does not apply to a person who owns an estate or interest in the premises and wholly occupies them unless, for the purpose of disposing of the premises, he—

    (a)   uses the services of an estate agent, or

    (b)   publishes an advertisement or causes an advertisement to be published.

   (3)   It is unlawful for a person managing any premises to discriminate against a disabled person occupying those premises—

    (a)   in the way he permits the disabled person to make use of any benefits or facilities;

    (b)   by refusing or deliberately omitting to permit the disabled person to make use of any benefits or facilities; or

    (c)   by evicting the disabled person, or subjecting him to any other detriment.

   (4)   It is unlawful for any person whose licence or consent is required for the disposal of any premises comprised in, or (in Scotland) the subject of, a tenancy to discriminate against a disabled person by withholding his licence or consent for the disposal of the premises to the disabled person.

   (5)   Subsection (4) applies to tenancies created before as well as after the passing of this Act.

   (6)   In this section—

    'advertisement' includes every form of advertisement or notice, whether to the public or not;

    'dispose', in relation to premises, includes granting a right to occupy the premises, and, in relation to premises comprised in, or (in Scotland) the subject of, a tenancy, includes—

    (a)   assigning the tenancy, and

    (b)   sub-letting or parting with possession of the premises or any part of the premises;

and 'disposal' shall be construed accordingly;

    'estate agent' means a person who, by way of profession or trade, provides services for the purpose of finding premises for persons seeking to acquire them or assisting in the disposal of premises; and

    'tenancy' means a tenancy created—

    (a)   by a lease or sub-lease,

    (b)   by an agreement for a lease or sub-lease,

    (c)   by a tenancy agreement, or

    (d)   in pursuance of any enactment.

   (7)   In the case of an act which constitutes discrimination by virtue of section 55, this section also applies to discrimination against a person who is not disabled.

   (8)   This section applies only in relation to premises in the United Kingdom.

23. Exemption for small dwellings

   (1)   Where the conditions mentioned in subsection (2) are satisfied, subsection (1), (3) or (as the case may be) (4) of section 22 does not apply.

   (2)   The conditions are that—

    (a)   the relevant occupier resides, and intends to continue to reside, on the premises;

    (b)   the relevant occupier shares accommodation on the premises with persons who reside on the premises and are not members of his household;

    (c)   the shared accommodation is not storage accommodation or a means of access; and

    (d)   the premises are small premises.

(3) For the purposes of this section, premises are 'small premises' if they fall within subsection (4) or (5).

(4) Premises fall within this subsection if—

(a) only the relevant occupier and members of his household reside in the accommodation occupied by him;

(b) the premises comprise, in addition to the accommodation occupied by the relevant occupier, residential accommodation for at least one other household;

(c) the residential accommodation for each other household is let, or available for letting, on a separate tenancy or similar agreement; and

(d) there are not normally more than two such other households.

(5) Premises fall within this subsection if there is not normally residential accommodation on the premises for more than six persons in addition to the relevant occupier and any members of his household.

(6) For the purposes of this section 'the relevant occupier' means—

(a) in a case falling within section 22(1), the person with power to dispose of the premises, or a near relative of his;

(b) in a case falling within section 22(4), the person whose licence or consent is required for the disposal of the premises, or a near relative of his.

(7) For the purposes of this section—

'near relative' means a person's spouse, partner, parent, child, grandparent, grandchild, or brother or sister (whether of full or half blood or by affinity); and

'partner' means the other member of a couple consisting of a man and a woman who are not married to each other but are living together as husband and wife.

24. Meaning of 'discrimination'

(1) For the purposes of section 22, a person ('A') discriminates against a disabled person if—

(a) for a reason which relates to the disabled person's disabilty, he treats him less favourably than he treats or would treat others to whom that reason does not or would not apply; and

(b) he cannot show that the treatment in question is justified.

(2) For the purposes of this section, treatment is justified only if—

(a) in A's opinion, one or more of the conditions mentioned in subsection (3) are satisfied; and

(b) it is reasonable, in all the circumstances of the case, for him to hold that opinion.

(3) The conditions are that—

(a) in any case, the treatment is necessary in order not to endanger the health or safety of any person (which may include that of the disabled person);

(b) in any case, the disabled person is incapable of entering into an enforceable agreement, or of giving an informed consent, and for that reason the treatment is reasonable in that case;

(c) in a case falling within section 22(3)(a), the treatment is necessary in order for the disabled person or the occupiers of other premises forming part of the building to make use of the benefit or facility;

(d) in a case falling within section 22(3)(b), the treatment is necessary in order for the occupiers of other premises forming part of the building to make use of the benefit or facility.

(4) Regulations may make provision, for purposes of this section, as to circumstances in which—

(a) it is reasonable for a person to hold the opinion mentioned in subsection 2(a);

(b) it is not reasonable for a person to hold that opinion.

(5) Regulations may make provision, for purposes of this section, as to circumstances (other than those mentioned in subsection (3)) in which treatment is to be taken to be justified.

Enforcement, etc.

25. Enforcement, remedies and procedure

(1) A claim by any person that another person—

(a) has discriminated against him in a way which is unlawful under this Part; or

(b) is by virtue of section 57 or 58 to be treated as having discriminated against him in such a way,

may be made the subject of civil proceedings in the same way as any other claim in tort or (in Scotland) in reparation for breach of statutory duty.

(2) For the avoidance of doubt it is hereby declared that damages in respect of discrimination in a way which is unlawful under this Part may include compensation for injury to feelings whether or not they include compensation under any other head.

(3) Proceedings in England and Wales shall be brought only in a county court.

(4) Proceedings in Scotland shall be brought only in a sheriff court.

(5) The remedies available in such proceedings are those which are available in the High Court or (as the case may be) the Court of Session.

(6) Part II of Schedule 3 makes further provision about the enforcement of this Part and about procedure.

26. Validity and revision of certain agreements

(1) Any term in a contract for the provision of goods, facilities or services or in any other agreement is void so far as it purports to—

(a) require a person to do anything which would contravene any provision of, or made under, this Part,

(b) exclude or limit the operation of any provision of this Part, or

(c) prevent any person from making a claim under this Part.

(2) Paragraph (b) and (c) of subsection (1) do not apply to an agreement settling a claim to which section 25 applies.

(3) On the application of any person interested in an agreement to which subsection (1) applies, a county court or a sheriff court may make such order as it thinks just for modifying the agreement to take account of the effect of subsection (1).

(4) No such order shall be made unless all persons affected have been—

(a) given notice of the application; and

(b) afforded an opportunity to make representations to the court.

(5) Subsection (4) applies subject to any rules of court providing for that notice to be dispensed with.

(6) An order under subsection (3) may include provision as respects any period befor the making of the order.

27. Alterations to premises occupied under leases

(1) This section applies where—

(a)   a provider of services ('the occupier') occupies premises under a lease;

(b)   but for this section, he would not be entitled to make a particular alteration to the premises; and

(c)   the alteration is one which the occupier proposes to make in order to comply with a section 21 duty.

(2)   Except to the extent to which it expressly so provides, the lease shall have effect by virtue of this subsection as if it provided—

(a)   for the occupier to be entitled to make the alteration with the written consent of the lessor;

(b)   for the occupier to have to make a written application to the lessor for consent if he wishes to make the alteration;

(c)   if such an application is made, for the lessor not to withhold his consent unreasonably; and

(d)   for the lessor to be entitled to make his consent subject to reasonable conditions.

(3)   In this section—

'lease' includes a tenancy, sub-lease or sub-tenancy and an agreement for a lease, tenancy, sub-lease or sub-tenancy; and

'sub-lease' and 'sub-tenancy' have such meaning as may be prescribed.

(4)   If the terms and conditions of a lease—

(a)   impose conditions which are to apply if the occupier alters the premises, or

(b)   entitle the lessor to impose conditions when consenting to the occupier's altering the premises,

the occupier is to be treated for the purposes of subsection (1) as not being entitled to make the alteration.

(5)   Part II of Schedule 4 supplements the provisions of this section.

28. Advice and assistance

(1)   The Secretary of State may make arrangements for the provision of advice and assistance to persons with a view to promoting the settlement of disputes arising under this Part otherwise than by recourse to the courts.

(2)   Any person appointed by the Secretary of State in connection with arrangements made under subsection (1) shall have such duties as the Secretary of State may direct.

(3)   The Secretary of State may pay to any person so appointed such allowances and compensation for loss of earnings as he considers appropriate.

(4)   The Secretary of State may make such payments, by way of grants, in respect of expenditure incurred, or to be incurred, by any person exercising functions in accordance with arrangements made by the Secretary of State under this section as he considers appropriate.

(5)   The approval of the Treasury is required for any payment under subsection (3) or (4).

PART IV   EDUCATION

29. Education of disabled persons

(1)   In section 161(5) of the Education Act 1993 (information relating to pupils with special educational needs to be included in annual report), omit the words from 'and in this subsection' to the end.

(2)   After section 161(5) of that Act insert—

'(6)   The annual report for each county, voluntary or grant-maintained school shall include a report containing information as to—

(a)   the arrangements for the admission of disabled pupils;

(b)   the steps taken to prevent disabled pupils from being treated less favourably than other pupils; and

(c)   the facilities provided to assist access to the school by disabled pupils.

(7)   In this section—

'annual report' means the report prepared under the articles of government for the school in accordance with section 30 of the Education (No. 2) Act 1986 or, as the case may be, paragraph 8 of Schedule 6 to this Act; and

'disabled pupils' means pupils who are disabled persons for the purposes of the Disability Discrimination Act 1995.'

(3)   In section 1 of the Education Act 1994 (establishment of the Teacher Training Agency) add, at the end—

'(4)   In exercising their functions, the Teacher Training Agency shall have regard to the requirements of persons who are disabled persons for the purposes of the Disability Discrimination Act 1995.'

30.   Further and higher education of disabled persons

(1)   The Further and Higher Education Act 1992 is amended as set out in subsections (2) to (6).

(2)   In section 5 (administration of funds by further education funding councils), in subsection (6)(b), after 'may' insert ', subject to subsection (7A) below,'.

(3)   After section 5(7) insert—

'(7A)   Without prejudice to the power to impose conditions given by subsection (6)(b) above, the conditions subject to which a council gives financial support under this section to the governing body of an institution within the further education sector—

(a)   shall require the governing body to publish disability statements at such intervals as may be prescribed; and

(b)   may include conditions relating to the provision made, or to be made, by the institution with respect to disabled persons.

(7B)   For the purposes of subsection (7A) above—

'disability statement' means a statement containing information of a prescribed description about the provision of facilities for education made by the institution in respect of disabled persons;

'disabled persons' means persons who are disabled persons for the purposes of the Disability Discrimination Act 1995; and

'prescribed' means prescribed by regulations.'

(4)   In section 8 (supplementary functions) add, at the end—

'(6)   As soon as is reasonably practicable after the end of its financial year, each council shall make a written report to the Secretary of State on—

(a)   the progress made during the year to which the report relates in the provision of further education for disabled students in their area; and

(b)   their plans for the future provision of further education for disabled students in their area.

(7)   In subsection (6) above—

'disabled students' means students who are disabled persons for the purposes of the Disability Discrimination Act 1995; and

'financial year' means the period of twelve months ending with 31st March 1997 and each successive period of twelve months.'

(5)   In section 62 (establishment of higher education funding councils), after subsection (7) insert—

'(7A)   In exercising their functions, each council shall have regard to the requirements of disabled persons.

(7B)   In subsection (7A) 'disabled persons' means persons who are disabled persons for the purposes of the Disability Discrimination Act 1995.'

(6)   In section 65 (administration of funds by higher education funding councils), after subsection (4) insert—

'(4A)   Without prejudice to the power to impose conditions given by subsection (3) above, the conditions subject to which a council makes grants, loans or other payments under this section to the governing body of a higher education institution shall require the governing body to publish disability statements at such intervals as may be specified.

(4B)   For the purposes of subsection (4A) above—

'disability statement' means a statement containing information of a specified description about the provision of facilities for education and research made by the institution in respect of persons who are disabled persons for the purposes of the Disability Discrimination Act 1995; and

'specified' means specified in the conditions subject to which grants, loans or other payments are made by a council under this section.'

(7)   The Education Act 1944 is amended as set out in subsection (8) and (9).

(8)   In section 41 (functions of local education authorities in respect of further education), after subsection (2) insert—

'(2A)   It shall be the duty of every local education authority to publish disability statements at such intervals as may be prescribed.

(2B)   For the purposes of subsection (2A) above—

'disability statement' means a statement containing information of a prescribed description about the provision of facilities for further education made by the local education authority in respect of persons who are disabled persons for the purposes of the Disability Discrimination Act 1995; and

'prescribed' means prescribed by regulations made by the Secretary of State.'

(9)   In section 41(7), (8) and (11), for 'this section' substitute 'subsections (1) and (6) above'.

31.   Further and higher education of disabled persons: Scotland

(1)   The Further and Higher Education (Scotland) Act 1992 is amended as follows.

(2)   In section 37 (establishment of Scottish Higher Education Funding Council) after subsection (4) insert—

'(4A)   In exercising their functions, the Council shall have regard to the requirements of disabled persons.

(4B)   In subsection (4A) above, 'disabled persons' means persons who are disabled persons for the purpose of the Disability Discrimination Act 1995.'

(3)   In section 40 (administration of funds by the Council), after subsection (4) insert—

'(5)   Without prejudice to the power to impose conditions given by subsection (3) above, the conditions subject to which the Council make grants, loans or other payments under this section to the governing body of an institution within the higher education sector shall require the governing body to publish disability statements at such intervals as may be specified.

(6)   For the purposes of subsection (5) above—

'disability statement' means a statement containing information of a specified description about the provision of facilities for education and research made by the institution in respect of persons who are disabled persons for the purpose of the Disability Discrimination Act 1995; and

'specified' means specified in the conditions subject to which grants, loans or other payments are made by the Council under this section.'

PART V   PUBLIC TRANSPORT

Taxis

32.   Taxi accessibility regulations

(1)   The Secretary of State may make regulations ('taxi accessibility regulations') for the purpose of securing that it is possible—

(a)   for disabled persons—

(i)   to get into and out of taxis in safety;

(ii)   to be carried in taxis in safety and in reasonable comfort; and

(b)   for disabled persons in wheelchairs—

(i)   to be conveyed in safety into and out of taxis while remaining in their wheelchairs; and

(ii)   to be carried in taxis in safety and in reasonable comfort while remaining in their wheelchairs.

(2)   Taxi accessibility regulations may, in particular—

(a)   require any regulated taxi to conform with provisions of the regulations as to—

(i)   the size of any door opening which is for the use of passengers;

(ii)   the floor area of the passenger compartment;

(iii)   the amount of headroom in the passenger compartment;

(iv)   the fitting of restraining devices designed to ensure the stability of a wheelchair while the taxi is moving;

(b)   require the driver of any regulated taxi which is plying for hire, or which has been hired, to comply with provisions of the regulations as to the carrying of ramps or other devices designed to facilitate the loading and unloading of wheelchairs;

(c)   require the driver of any regulated taxi in which a disabled person who is in a wheelchair is being carried (while remaining in his wheelchair) to comply with provisions of the regulations as to the position in which the wheelchair is to be secured.

(3)   The driver of a regulated taxi which is plying for hire, or which has been hired, is guilty of an offence if—

(a)   he fails to comply with any requirement imposed on him by the regulations; or

(b)   the taxi fails to conform with any provision of the regulations with which it is required to conform.

(4)   A person who is guilty of such an offence is liable, on summary conviction, to a fine not exceeding level 3 on the standard scale.

(5)   In this section—

'passenger compartment' has such meaning as may be prescribed;

'regulated taxi' means any taxi to which the regulations are expressed to apply;

'taxi' means a vehicle licensed under—

(a)   section 37 of the Town Police Clauses Act 1847, or

(b)   section 6 of the Metropolitan Public Carriage Act 1869,

but does not include a taxi which is drawn by a horse or other animal.

33.   Designated transport facilities

(1)   In this section 'a franchise agreement' means a contract entered into by the operator of a designated transport facility for the provision by the other party to the contract of hire car services—

(a)   for members of the public using any part of the transport facility; and

(b)   which involve vehicles entering any part of that facility.

(2)   The Secretary of State may by regulations provide for the application of any taxi provision in relation to—

(a)   vehicles used for the provision of services under a franchise agreement; or

(b)   the drivers of such vehicles.

(3)   Any regulations under subsection (2) may apply any taxi provision with such modifications as the Secretary of State considers appropriate.

(4)   In this section—

'designated' means designated for the purposes of this section by an order made by the Secretary of State;

'hire car' has such meaning as may be prescribed;

'operator', in relation to a transport facility, means any person who is concerned with the management or operation of the facility;

'taxi provision' means any provision of—

(a)   this Act, or

(b)   regulations made in pursuance of section 20(2A) of the Civic Government (Scotland) Act 1982,

which applies in relation to taxis or the drivers of taxis; and

'transport facility' means any premises which form part of any port, airport, railway station or bus station.

34.   New licences conditional on compliance with taxi accessibility regulations

(1)   No licensing authority shall grant a licence for a taxi to ply for hire unless the vehicle conforms with those provisions of the taxi accessibility regulations with which it will be required to conform if licensed.

(2)   Subsection (1) does not apply if such a licence was in force with respect to the vehicle at any time during the period of 28 days immediately before the day on which the licence is granted.

(3)   The Secretary of State may by order provide for subsection (2) to cease to have effect on such date as may be specified in the order.

(4)   Separate orders may be made under subsection (3) with respect to different areas or localities.

35. Exemption from taxi accessibility regulations

(1)   The Secretary of State may make regulations ('exemption regulations') for the purpose of enabling any relevant licensing authority to apply to him for an order (an 'exemption order') exempting the authority from the requirements of section 34.

(2)   Exemption regulations may, in particular, make provision requiring a licensing authority proposing to apply for an exemption order—

(a)   to carry out such consultations as may be prescribed;

(b)   to publish the proposal in the prescribed manner;

(c)   to consider any representations made to it about the proposal, before applying for the order;

(d)   to make its application in the prescribed form.

(3)   A licensing authority may apply for an exemption order only if it is satisfied—

(a)   that, having regard to the circumstances prevailing in its area, it would be inappropriate for the requirements of section 34 to apply; and

(b)   that the application of section 34 would result in an unacceptable reduction in the number of taxis in its area.

(4)   After considering any application for an exemption order and consulting the Disabled Persons Transport Advisory Committee and such other persons as he considers appropriate, the Secretary of State may—

(a)   make an exemption order in the terms of the application;

(b)   make an exemption order in such other terms as he considers appropriate; or

(c)   refuse to make an exemption order.

(5)   The Secretary of State may by regulations ('swivel seat regulations') make provision requiring any exempt taxi plying for hire in an area in respect of which an exemption order is in force to conform with provisions of the regulations as to the fitting and use of swivel seats.

(6)   The Secretary of State may by regulations make provision with respect to swivel seat regulations similar to that made by section 34 with respect to taxi accessibility regulations.

(7)   In this section—

'exempt taxi' means a taxi in relation to which section 34(1) would apply if the exemption order were not in force;

'relevant licensing authority' means a licensing authority responsible for licensing taxis in any area of England and Wales other than the area to which the Metropolitan Public Carriage Act 1869 applies; and

'swivel seats' has such meaning as may be prescribed.

36. Carrying of passengers in wheelchairs

(1)   This section imposes duties on the driver of a regulated taxi which has been hired—

(a)   by or for a disabled person who is in a wheelchair; or

(b)   by a person who wishes such a disabled person to accompany him in the taxi.

(2)   In this section—

'carry' means carry in the taxi concerned; and

'the passenger' means the disabled person concerned.

(3)   The duties are—

(a)   to carry the passenger while he remains in his wheelchair;

(b)   not to make any additional charge for doing so;

(c)   if the passenger chooses to sit in a passenger seat, to carry the wheelchair;

(d)   to take such steps as are necessary to ensure that the passenger is carried in safety and in reasonable comfort;

(e)   to give such assistance as may be reasonably required—

(i)   to enable the passenger to get into or out of the taxi;

(ii)   if the passenger wishes to remain in his wheelchair, to enable him to be conveyed into and out of the taxi while in his wheelchair;

(iii)   to load the passenger's luggage into or out of the taxi;

(iv)   if the passenger does not wish to remain in his wheelchair, to load the wheelchair into or out of the taxi.

(4)   Nothing in this section is to be taken to require the driver of any taxi—

(a)   except in the case of a taxi of a prescribed description, to carry more than one person in a wheelchair, or more than one wheelchair, on any one journey; or

(b)   to carry any person in circumstances in which it would otherwise be lawful for him to refuse to carry that person.

(5)   A driver of a regulated taxi who fails to comply with any duty imposed on him by this section is guilty of an offence and liable, on summary conviction, to a fine not exceeding level 3 on the standard scale.

(6)   In any proceedings for an offence under this section, it is a defence for the accused to show that, even though at the time of the alleged offence the taxi conformed with those provisions of the taxi accessibility regulations with which it was required to conform, it would not have been possible for the wheelchair in question to be carried in safety in the taxi.

(7)   If the licensing authority is satisfied that it is appropriate to exempt a person from the duties imposed by this section—

(a)   on medical grounds, or

(b)   on the ground that his physical condition makes it impossible or unreasonably difficult for him to comply with the duties imposed on drivers by this section,

it shall issue him with a certificate of exemption.

(8)   A certificate of exemption shall be issued for such period as may be specified in the certificate.

(9)   The driver of a regulated taxi is exempt from the duties imposed by this section if—

(a)   a certificate of exemption issued to him under this section is in force; and

(b)   the prescribed notice of his exemption is exhibited on the taxi in the prescribed manner.

37.   Carrying of guide dogs and hearing dogs

(1)   This section imposes duties on the driver of a taxi which has been hired—

(a)   by or for a disabled person who is accompanied by his guide dog or hearing dog, or

(b)   by a person who wishes such a disabled person to accompany him in the taxi.

(2)   The disabled person is referred to in this section as 'the passenger'.

(3)   The duties are—

(a)   to carry the passenger's dog and allow it to remain with the passenger; and

(b)   not to make any additional charge for doing so.

(4)   A driver of a taxi who fails to comply with any duty imposed on him by this section is guilty of an offence and liable, on summary conviction, to a fine not exceeding level 3 on the standard scale.

(5)   If the licensing authority is satisfied that it is appropriate on medical grounds to exempt a person from the duties imposed by this section, it shall issue him with a certificate of exemption.

(6)   In determining whether to issue a certificate of exemption, the licensing authority shall, in particular, have regard to the physical characteristics of the taxi which the applicant drives or those of any kind of taxi in relation to which he requires the certificate.

(7)   A certificate of exemption shall be issued—

(a)   with respect to a specified taxi or a specified kind of taxi; and

(b)   for such period as may be specified in the certificate.

(8)   The driver of a taxi is exempt from the duties imposed by this section if—

(a)   a certificate of exemption issued to him under this section is in force with respect to the taxi; and

(b)   the prescribed notice of his exemption is exhibited on the taxi in the prescribed manner.

(9)   The Secretary of State may, for the purposes of this section, prescribe any other category of dog trained to assist a disabled person who has a disability of a prescribed kind.

(10)   This section applies in relation to any such prescribed category of dog as it applies in relation to guide dogs.

(11)   In this section—

'guide dog' means a dog which has been trained to guide a blind person; and

'hearing dog' means a dog which has been trained to assist a deaf person.

38.   Appeal against refusal of exemption certificate

(1)   Any person who is aggrieved by the refusal of a licensing authority to issue an exemption certificate under section 36 or 37 may appeal to the appropriate court before the end of the period of 28 days beginning with the date of the refusal.

(2)   On an appeal to it under this section, the court may direct the licensing authority concerned to issue the appropriate certificate of exemption to have effect for such period as may be specified in the direction.

(3)   'Appropriate court' means the magistrates' court for the petty sessions area in which the licensing authority has its principal office.

39.   Requirements as to disabled passengers in Scotland

(1)   Part II of the Civic Government (Scotland) Act 1982 (licensing and regulation) is amended as follows.

(2)   In subsection (4) of section 10 (suitability of vehicle for use as taxi)—

(a)   after 'authority' insert '—(a)'; and

(b)   at the end add '; and

    (b)   as not being so suitable if it does not so comply.'

(3)   In section 20 (regulations relating to taxis etc.) after subsection (2) insert—

'(2A)   Without prejudice to the generality of subsections (1) and (2) above, regulations under those subsections may make such provision as appears to the Secretary of State to be necessary or expedient in relation to the carrying in taxis of disabled persons (within the meaning of section 1(2) of the Disability Discrimination Act 1995) and such provision may in particular prescribe—

    (a)   requirements as to the carriage of wheelchairs, guide dogs, hearing dogs and other categories of dog;

    (b)   a date from which any such provision is to apply and the extent to which it is to apply; and

    (c)   the circumstances in which an exemption from such provision may be granted in respect of any taxi or taxi driver,

and in this subsection—

       'guide dog' means a dog which has been trained to guide a blind person;

       'hearing dog' means a dog which has been trained to assist a deaf person; and

       'other categories of dog' means such other categories of dog as the Secretary of State may prescribe, trained to assist disabled persons who have disabilities of such kinds as he may prescribe.'

Public service vehicles

40. PSV accessibility regulations

(1)   The Secretary of State may make regulations ('PSV accessibility regulations') for the purpose of securing that it is possible for disabled persons—

    (a)   to get on to and off regulated public service vehicles in safety and without unreasonable difficulty (and, in the case of disabled persons in wheelchairs, to do so while remaining in their wheelchairs); and

    (b)   to be carried in such vehicles in safety and in reasonable comfort.

(2)   PSV accessibility regulations may, in particular, make provision as to the construction, use and maintenance of regulated public service vehicles including provision as to—

    (a)   the fitting of equipment to vehicles;

    (b)   equipment to be carried by vehicles;

    (c)   the design of equipment to be fitted to, or carried by, vehicles;

    (d)   the fitting and use of restraining devices designed to ensure the stability of wheelchairs while vehicles are moving;

    (e)   the position in which wheelchairs are to be secured while vehicles are moving.

(3)   Any person who—

    (a)   contravenes or fails to comply with any provision of the PSV accessibility regulations,

    (b)   uses on a road a regulated public service vehicle which does not conform with any provision of the regulations with which it is required to conform, or

    (c)   causes or permits to be used on a road such a regulated public service vehicle, is guilty of an offence.

(4)   A person who is guilty of such an offence is liable, on summary conviction, to a fine not exceeding level 4 on the standard scale.

(5)   In this section—
'public service vehicle' means a vehicle which is—
(a)   adapted to carry more than eight passengers; and
(b)   a public service vehicle for the purposes of the Public Passenger Vehicles Act 1981;
'regulated public service vehicle' means any public service vehicle to which the PSV accessibility regulations are expressed to apply.
(6)   Different provision may be made in regulations under this section—
(a)   as respects different classes or descriptions of vehicle;
(b)   as respects the same class or description of vehicle in different circumstances.
(7)   Before making any regulations under this section or section 41 or 42 the Secretary of State shall consult the Disabled Persons Transport Advisory Committee and such other representative organisations as he thinks fit.

41.   Accessibility certificates

(1)   A regulated public service vehicle shall not be used on a road unless—
(a)   a vehicle examiner has issued a certificate (as 'accessibility certificate') that such provisions of the PSV accessibility regulations as may be prescribed are satisfied in respect of the vehicle; or
(b)   an approval certificate has been issued under section 42 in respect of the vehicle.
(2)   The Secretary of State may make regulations—
(a)   with respect to applications for, and the issue of, accessibility certificates;
(b)   providing for the examination of vehicles in respect of which applications have been made;
(c)   with respect to the issue of copies of accessibility certificates in place of certificates which have been lost or destroyed.
(3)   If a regulated public service vehicle is used in contravention of this section, the operator of the vehicle is guilty of an offence and liable on summary conviction to a fine not exceeding level 4 on the standard scale.
(4)   In this section 'operator' has the same meaning as in the Public Passenger Vehicles Act 1981.

42.   Approval certificates

(1)   Where the Secretary of State is satisfied that such provisions of the PSV accessibility regulations as may be prescribed for the purposes of section 41 are satisfied in respect of a particular vehicle he may approve the vehicle for the purposes of this section.
(2)   A vehicle which has been so approved is referred to in this section as a 'type vehicle'.
(3)   Subsection (4) applies where a declaration in the prescribed form has been made by an authorised person that a particular vehicle conforms in design, construction and equipment with a type vehicle.
(4)   A vehicle examiner may, after examining (if he thinks fit) the vehicle to which the declaration applies, issue a certificate in the prescribed form ('an approval certificate') that it conforms to the type vehicle.
(5)   The Secretary of State may make regulations—
(a)   with respect to applications for, and grants of, approval under subsection (1);

(b) with respect to applications for, and the issue of, approval certificates;

(c) providing for the examination of vehicles in respect of which applications have been made;

(d) with respect to the issue of copies of approval certificates in place of certificates which have been lost or destroyed.

(6) The Secretary of State may at any time withdraw his approval of a type vehicle.

(7) Where an approval is withdrawn—

(a) no further approval certificates shall be issued by reference to the type vehicle; but

(b) any approval certificate issued by reference to the type vehicle before the withdrawal shall continue to have effect for the purposes of section 41.

(8) In subsection (3) 'authorised person' means a person authorised by the Secretary of State for the purposes of that subsection.

43. Special authorisations

(1) The Secretary of State may by order authorise the use on roads of—

(a) any regulated public service vehicle of a class or description specified by the order, or

(b) any regulated public service vehicle which is so specified,

and nothing in section 40, 41 or 42 prevents the use of any vehicle in accordance with the order.

(2) Any such authorisation may be given subject to such restrictions and conditions as may be specified by or under the order.

(3) The Secretary of State may by order make provision for the purpose of securing that, subject to such restrictions and conditions as may be specified by or under the order, provisions of the PSV accessibility regulations apply to regulated public service vehicles of a description specified by the order subject to such modifications or exceptions as may be specified by the order.

44. Review and appeals

(1) Subsection (2) applies where—

(a) the Secretary of State refuses an application for the approval of a vehicle under section 42(1); and

(b) before the end of the prescribed period, the applicant asks the Secretary of State to review the decision and pays any fee fixed under section 45.

(2) The Secretary of State shall—

(a) review the decision; and

(b) in doing so, consider any representations made to him in writing, before the end of the prescribed period, by the applicant.

(3) A person applying for an accessibility certificate or an approval certificate may appeal to the Secretary of State against the refusal of a vehicle examiner to issue such a certificate.

(4) An appeal must be made within the prescribed time and in the prescribed manner.

(5) Regulations may make provision as to the procedure to be followed in connection with appeals.

(6) On the determination of an appeal, the Secretary of State may—

(a) confirm, vary or reverse the decision appealed against;

(b)   give such directions as he thinks fit to the vehicle examiner for giving effect to his decision.

45.   Fees

(1)   Such fees, payable at such times, as may be prescribed may be charged by the Secretary of State in respect of—

(a)   applications for, and grants of, approval under section 42(1);

(b)   applications for, and the issue of, accessibility certificates and approval certificates;

(c)   copies of such certificates;

(d)   reviews and appeals under section 44.

(2)   Any such fees received by the Secretary of State shall be paid by him into the Consolidated Fund.

(3)   Regulations under subsection (1) may make provision for the repayment of fees, in whole or in part, in such circumstances as may be prescribed.

(4)   Before making any regulations under subsection (1) the Secretary of State shall consult such representative organisations as he thinks fit.

Rail vehicles

46.   Rail vehicle accessibility regulations

(1)   The Secretary of State may make regulations ('rail vehicle accessibility regulations') for the purpose of securing that it is possible—

(a)   for disabled persons—

(i)   to get on to and off regulated rail vehicles in safety and without unreasonable difficulty;

(ii)   to be carried in such vehicles in safety and in reasonable comfort; and

(b)   for disabled persons in wheelchairs—

(i)   to get on to and off such vehicles in safety and without unreasonable difficulty while remaining in their wheelchairs, and

(ii)   to be carried in such vehicles in safety and in reasonable comfort while remaining in their wheelchairs.

(2)   Rail vehicle accessibility regulations may, in particular, make provision as to the construction, use and maintenance of regulated rail vehicles including provision as to—

(a)   the fitting of equipment to vehicles;

(b)   equipment to be carried by vehicles;

(c)   the design of equipment to be fitted to, or carried by, vehicles;

(d)   the use of equipment fitted to, or carried by, vehicles;

(e)   the toilet facilities to be provided in vehicles;

(f)   the location and floor area of the wheelchair accommodation to be provided in vehicles;

(g)   assistance to be given to disabled persons.

(3)   If a regulated rail vehicle which does not conform with any provision of the rail vehicle accessibility regulations with which it is required to conform is used for carriage, the operator of the vehicle is guilty of an offence.

(4)   A person who is guilty of such an offence is liable, on summary conviction, to a fine not exceeding level 4 on the standard scale.

(5)   Different provision may be made in rail vehicle accessibility regulations—

(a)   as respects different classes or descriptions of rail vehicle;

(b)   as respects the same class or description of rail vehicle in different circumstances;

(c)   as respects different networks.

(6)   In this section—

'network' means any permanent way or other means of guiding or supporting rail vehicles or any section of it;

'operator', in relation to any rail vehicle, means the person having the management of that vehicle;

'rail vehicle' means a vehicle—

(a)   constructed or adapted to carry passengers on any railway, tramway or prescribed system; and

(b)   first brought into use, or belonging to a class of vehicle first brought into use, after 31st December 1998;

'regulated rail vehicle' means any rail vehicle to which the rail vehicle accessibility regulations are expressed to apply; and

'wheelchair accommodation' has such meaning as may be prescribed.

(7)   In subsection (6)—

'prescribed system' means a system using a prescribed mode of guided transport ('guided transport' having the same meaning as in the Transport and Works Act 1992); and

'railway' and 'tramway' have the same meaning as in that Act.

(8)   The Secretary of State may by regulations make provision as to the time when a rail vehicle, or a class of rail vehicle, is to be treated, for the purposes of this section, as first brought into use.

(9)   Regulations under subsection (8) may include provision for disregarding periods of testing and other prescribed periods of use.

(10)   For the purposes of this section and section 47, a person uses a vehicle for carriage if he uses it for the carriage of members of the public for hire or reward at separate fares.

(11)   Before making any regulations under subsection (1) or section 47 the Secretary of State shall consult the Disabled Persons Transport Advisory Committee and such other representative organisations as he thinks fit.

47.   Exemption from rail vehicle accessibility regulations

(1)   The Secretary of State may by order (an 'exemption order') authorise the use for carriage of any regulated rail vehicle of a specified description, or in specified circumstances, even though that vehicle does not conform with the provisions of the rail vehicle accessibility regulations with which it is required to conform.

(2)   Regulations may make provision with respect to exemption orders including, in particular, provision as to—

(a)   the persons by whom applications for exemption orders may be made;

(b)   the form in which such applications are to be made;

(c)   information to be supplied in connection with such applications;

(d)   the period for which exemption orders are to continue in force;

(e)   the revocation of exemption orders.

(3)   After considering any application for an exemption order and consulting the Disabled Persons Transport Advisory Committee and such other persons as he considers appropriate, the Secretary of State may—

(a) make an exemption order in the terms of the application;

(b) make an exemption order in such other terms as he considers appropriate;

(c) refuse to make an exemption order.

(4) An exemption order may be made subject to such restrictions and conditions as may be specified.

(5) In this section 'specified' means specified in an exemption order.

Supplemental

48. Offences by bodies corporate etc.

(1) Where an offence under section 40 or 46 committed by a body corporate is committed with the consent or connivance of, or is attributable to any neglect on the part of, a director, manager, secretary or other similar officer of the body, or a person purporting to act in such a capacity, he as well as the body corporate is guilty of the offence.

(2) In subsection (1) 'director', in relation to a body corporate whose affairs are managed by its members, means a member of the body corporate.

(3) Where, in Scotland, an offence under section 40 or 46 committed by a partnership or by an unincorporated association other than a partnership is committed with the consent or connivance of, or is attributable to any neglect on the part of, a partner in the partnership or (as the case may be) a person concerned in the management or control of the association, he, as well as the partnership or association, is guilty of the offence.

49. Forgery and false statements

(1) In this section 'relevant document' means—

(a) a certificate of exemption issued under section 36 or 37;

(b) a notice of a kind mentioned in section 36(9)(b) or 37(8)(b);

(c) an accessibility certificate; or

(d) an approval certificate.

(2) A person is guilty of an offence if, with intent to deceive, he—

(a) forges, alters or uses a relevant document;

(b) lends a relevant document to any other person;

(c) allows a relevant document to be used by any other person; or

(d) makes or has in his possession any document which closely resembles a relevant document.

(3) A person who is guilty of an offence under subsection (2) is liable—

(a) on summary conviction, to a fine not exceeding the statutory maximum;

(b) on conviction on indictment, to imprisonment for a term not exceeding two years or to a fine or to both.

(4) A person who knowingly makes a false statement for the purpose of obtaining an accessibility certificate or an approval certificate is guilty of an offence and liable on summary conviction to a fine not exceeding level 4 on the standard scale.

PART VI   THE NATIONAL DISABILITY COUNCIL

50. The National Disability Council

(1) There shall be a body to be known as the National Disability Council (but in this Act referred to as 'the Council').

(2) It shall be the duty of the Council to advice the Secretary of State, either on its own initiative or when asked to do so by the Secretary of State—

(a) on matters relevant to the elimination of discrimination against disabled persons and persons who have had a disability;

(b) on measures which are likely to reduce or eliminate such discrimination; and

(c) on matters related to the operation of this Act or of provisions made under this Act.

(3) The Secretary of State may by order confer additional functions on the Council.

(4) The power conferred by subsection (3) does not include power to confer on the Council any functions with respect to the investigation of any complaint which may be the subject of proceedings under this Act.

(5) In discharging its duties under this section, the Council shall in particular have regard to—

(a) the extent and nature of the benefits which would be likely to result from the implementation of any recommendation which it makes; and

(b) the likely cost of implementing any such recommendation.

(6) Where the Council makes any recommendation in the discharge of any of its functions under this section it shall, if it is reasonably practicable to do so, make an assessment of—

(a) the likely cost of implementing the recommendation; and

(b) the likely financial benefits which would result from implementing it.

(7) Where the Council proposes to give the Secretary of State advice on a matter, it shall before doing so—

(a) consult any body—

(i) established by any enactment or by a Minister of the Crown for the purpose of giving advice in relation to disability, or any aspect of disability; and

(ii) having functions in relation to the matter to which the advice relates;

(b) consult such other persons as it considers appropriate; and

(c) have regard to any representations made to it as a result of any such consultations.

(8) Schedule 5 makes further provision with respect to the Council, including provision about its membership

(9) The power conferred on the Council by subsection (2) to give advice on its own initiative does not include power to give advice—

(a) by virtue of paragraph (a) or (b), in respect of any matter which relates to the operation of any provision of or arrangements made under—

(i) the Disabled Persons (Employment) Acts 1944 and 1958;

(ii) the Employment and Training Act 1973;

(iii) the Employment Protection (Consolidation) Act 1978; or

(iv) section 2(3) of the Enterprise and New Towns (Scotland) Act 1990; or

(b) by virtue of paragraph (c), in respect of any matter arising under Part II or section 53, 54, 56 or 61.

(10) Subsection (9) shall not have effect at any time when there is neither a national advisory council established under section 17(1)(a) of the Disabled Persons (Employment) Act 1944 nor any person appointed to act generally under section 60(1) of this Act.

51. Codes of practice prepared by the Council

(1) It shall be the duty of the council, when asked to do so by the Secretary of State—

(a) to prepare proposals for a code of practice dealing with the matters to which the Secretary of State's request relates; or

(b) to review a code and, if it considers it appropriate, propose alterations.

(2) The Secretary of State may, in accordance with the procedural provisions of section 52, issue codes of practice in response to proposals made by the Council under this section.

(3) A failure on the part of any person to observe any provision of a code does not of itself make that person liable to any proceedings.

(4) A code is admissible in evidence in any proceedings under this Act before an industrial tribunal, a county court or a sheriff court.

(5) If any provision of a code appears to a tribunal or court to be relevant to any question arising in any proceedings under this Act, it shall be taken into account in determining that question.

(6) In this section and section 52 'code' means a code issued by the Secretary of State under this section and includes a code which has been altered and re-issued.

52. Further provision about codes issued under section 51

(1) In this section 'proposal' means a proposal made by the Council to the Secretary of State under section 51.

(2) In preparing any proposal, the Council shall consult—

(a) such persons (if any) as the Secretary of State has specified in making his request to the Council; and

(b) such other persons (if any) as the Council considers appropriate.

(3) Before making any proposal, the Council shall publish a draft, consider any representations made to it about the draft and, if it thinks it appropriate, modify its proposal in the light of any of those representations.

(4) Where the Council makes any proposal, the Secretary of State may—

(a) approve it;

(b) approve it subject to such modifications as he considers appropriate; or

(c) refuse to approve it.

(5) Where the Secretary of State approves any proposal (with or without modifications), he shall prepare a draft of the proposed code and lay it before each House of Parliament.

(6) If, within the 40-day period, either House resolves not to approve the draft, the Secretary of State shall take no further steps in relation to the proposed code.

(7) If no such resolution is made within the 40-day period, the Secretary of State shall issue the code in the form of his draft.

(8) The code shall come into force on such date as the Secretary of State may appoint by order.

(9) Subsection (6) does not prevent a new draft of the proposed code from being laid before Parliament.

(10) If the Secretary of State refuses to approve a proposal, he shall give the Council a written statement of his reasons for not approving it.

(11) The Secretary of State may by order revoke a code.

(12) In this section '40-day period', in relation to the draft of a proposed code, means—

(a)   if the draft is laid before one House on a day later than the day on which it is laid before the other House, the period of 40 days beginning with the later of the two days, and

(b)   in any other case, the period of 40 days beginning with the day on which the draft is laid before each House,
no account being taken of any period during which Parliament is dissolved or prorogued or during which both Houses are adjourned for more than four days.

PART VII   SUPPLEMENTAL

53.   Codes of practice prepared by the Secretary of State

(1)   The Secretary of State may issue codes of practice containing such practical guidance as he considers appropriate with a view to—

(a)   eliminating discrimination in the field of employment against disabled persons and persons who have had a disability; or

(b)   encouraging good practice in relation to the employment of disabled persons and persons who have had a disability.

(2)   The Secretary of State may from time to time revise the whole or any part of a code and re-issue it.

(3)   Without prejudice to subsection (1), a code may include practical guidance as to—

(a)   the circumstances in which it would be reasonable, having regard in particular to the costs involved, for a person to be expected to make adjustments in favour of a disabled person or a person who has had a disability; or

(b)   what steps it is reasonably practicable for employers to take for the purpose of preventing their employees from doing, in the course of their employment, anything which is made unlawful by this Act.

(4)   A failure on the part of any person to observe any provision of a code does not of itself make that person liable to any proceedings.

(5)   A code is admissible in evidence in any proceedings under this Act before an industrial tribunal, a county court or a sheriff court.

(6)   If any provision of a code appears to a tribunal or court to be relevant to any question arising in any proceedings under this Act, it shall be taken into account in determining that question.

(7)   In this section and section 54 'code' means a code issued by the Secretary of State under this section and includes a code which has been revised and re-issued.

(8)   In subsection (1)(a), 'discrimination in the field of employment' includes discrimination of a kind mentioned in section 12 or 13.

(9)   In subsections (1)(b) and (3), 'employment' includes contract work (as defined by section 12(6)).

54.   Further provision about codes issued under section 53

(1)   In preparing a draft of any code under section 53, the Secretary of State shall consult such organisations representing the interests of employers or of disabled persons in, or seeking, employment as he considers appropriate.

(2)   Where the Secretary of State proposes to issue a code, he shall publish a draft of it, consider any representations that are made to him about the draft and, if he thinks it appropriate, modify his proposals in the light of any of those representations.

(3)   If the Secretary of State decides to proceed with a proposed code, he shall lay a draft of it before each House of Parliament.

(4)   If, within the 40-day period, either House resolves not to approve the draft, the Secretary of State shall take no further steps in relation to the proposed code.

(5)   If no such resolution is made within the 40-day period, the Secretary of State shall issue the code in the form of his draft.

(6)   The code shall come into force on such date as the Secretary of State may appoint by order.

(7)   Subsection (4) does not prevent a new draft of the proposed code from being laid before Parliament.

(8)   The Secretary of State may by order revoke a code.

(9)   In this section '40-day period', in relation to the draft of a proposed code, means—

(a)   if the draft is laid before one House on a day later than the day on which it is laid before the other House, the period of 40 days beginning with the later of the two days, and

(b)   in any other case, the period of 40 days beginning with the day on which the draft is laid before each House,

no account being taken of any period during which Parliament is dissolved or prorogued or during which both Houses are adjourned for more than four days.

55.   Victimisation

(1)   For the purposes of Part II or Part III, a person ('A') discriminates against another person ('B') if—

(a)   he treats B less favourably than he treats or would treat other persons whose circumstances are the same as B's; and

(b)   he does so for a reason mentioned in subsection (2).

(2)   The reasons are that—

(a)   B has—

(i)   brought proceedings against A or any other person under this Act; or

(ii)   given evidence or information in connection with such proceedings brought by any person; or

(iii)   otherwise done anything under this Act in relation to A or any other person; or

(iv)   alleged that A or any other person has (whether or not the allegation so states) contravened this Act, or

(b)   A believes or suspects that B has done or intends to do any of those things.

(3)   Where B is a disabled person, or a person who has had a disability, the disability in question shall be disregarded in comparing his circumstances with those of any other person for the purposes of subsection (1)(a).

(4)   Subsection (1) does not apply to treatment of a person because of an allegation made by him if the allegation was false and not made in good faith.

56.   Help for persons suffering discrimination

(1)   For the purposes of this section—

(a)   a person who considers that he may have been discriminated against, in contravention of any provision of Part II, is referred to as 'the complainant'; and

(b)   a person against whom the complainant may decide to make, or has made, a complaint under Part II is referred to as 'the respondent'.

(2)   The Secretary of State shall, with a view to helping the complainant to decide whether to make a complaint against the respondent and, if he does so, to formulate and present his case in the most effective manner, by order prescribe—

(a)   forms by which the complainant may question the respondent on his reasons for doing any relevant act, or on any other matter which is or may be relevant; and

(b)   forms by which the respondent may if he so wishes reply to any questions.

(3)   Where the complainant questions the respondent in accordance with forms prescribed by an order under subsection (2)—

(a)   the question, and any reply by the respondent (whether in accordance with such an order or not), shall be admissible as evidence in any proceedings under Part II;

(b)   if it appears to the tribunal in any such proceedings—

(i)   that the respondent deliberately, and without reasonable excuse, omitted to reply within a reasonable period, or

(ii)   that the respondent's reply is evasive or equivocal,

it may draw any inference which it considers it just and equitable to draw, including an inference that the respondent has contravened a provision of Part II.

(4)   The Secretary of State may by order prescribe—

(a)   the period within which questions must be duly served in order to be admissible under subsection (3)(a); and

(b)   the manner in which a question, and any reply by the respondent, may be duly served.

(5)   This section is without prejudice to any other enactment or rule of law regulating interlocutory and preliminary matters in proceedings before an industrial tribunal, and has effect subject to any enactment or rule of law regulating the admissibility of evidence in such proceedings.

57.   Aiding unlawful acts

(1)   A person who knowingly aids another person to do an act made unlawful by this Act is to be treated for the purposes of this Act as himself doing the same kind of unlawful act.

(2)   For the purposes of subsection (1), an employee or agent for whose act the employer or principal is liable under section 58 (or would be so liable but for section 58(5)) shall be taken to have aided the employer or principal to do the act.

(3)   For the purposes of this section, a person does not knowingly aid another to do an unlawful act if—

(a)   he acts in reliance on a statement made to him by that other person that, because of any provision of this Act, the act would not be unlawful; and

(b)   it is reasonable for him to rely on the statement.

(4)   A person who knowingly or recklessly makes such a statement which is false or misleading in a material respect if guilty of an offence.

(5)   Any person guilty of an offence under subsection (4) shall be liable on summary conviction to a fine not exceeding level 5 on the standard scale.

58.   Liability of employers and principals

(1)   Anything done by a person in the course of his employment shall be treated for the purposes of this Act as also done by his employer, whether or not it was done with the employer's knowledge or approval.

(2)   Anything done by a person as agent for another person with the authority of that other person shall be treated for the purposes of this Act as also done by that other person.

(3)   Subsection (2) applies whether the authority was—
    (a)   express or implied; or
    (b)   given before or after the act in question was done.
(4)   Subsections (1) and (2) do not apply in relation to an offence under section 57(4).
(5)   In proceedings under this Act against any person in respect of an act alleged to have been done by an employee of his, it shall be a defence for that person to prove that he took such steps as were reasonably practicable to prevent the employee from—
    (a)   doing that act; or
    (b)   doing, in the course of his employment, acts of that description.

59.   Statutory authority and national security etc.

(1)   Nothing in this Act makes unlawful any act done—
    (a)   in pursuance of any enactment; or
    (b)   in pursuance of any instrument made by a Minister of the Crown under any enactment; or
    (c)   to comply with any condition or requirement imposed by a Minister of the Crown (whether before or after the passing of this Act) by virtue of any enactment.
(2)   In subsection (1) 'enactment' includes one passed or made after the date on which this Act is passed and 'instrument' includes one made after that date.
(3)   Nothing in this Act makes unlawful any act done for the purpose of safeguarding national security.

PART VIII   MISCELLANEOUS

60.   Appointment by Secretary of State of advisers

(1)   The Secretary of State may appoint such persons as he thinks fit to advise or assist him in connection with matters relating to the employment of disabled persons and persons who have had a disability.
(2)   Persons may be appointed by the Secretary of State to act generally or in relation to a particular area or locality.
(3)   The Secretary of State may pay to any person appointed under this section such allowances and compensation for loss of earnings as he considers appropriate.
(4)   The approval of the Treasury is required for any payment under this section.
(5)   In subsection (1) 'employment' includes self-employment.
(6)   The Secretary of State may by order—
    (a)   provide for section 17 of, and Schedule 2 to, the Disabled Persons (Employment) Act 1944 (national advisory council and district advisory committees) to cease to have effect—
        (i)   so far as concerns the national advisory council; or
        (ii)   so far as concerns district advisory committees; or
    (b)   repeal that section and Schedule.
(7)   At any time before the coming into force of an order under paragraph (b) of subsection (6), section 17 of the Act of 1944 shall have effect as if in subsection (1), after 'disabled persons' in each case there were inserted ', and persons who have had a disability,' and as if at the end of the section there were added—
    '(3)   For the purposes of this section—
        (a)   a person is a disabled person if he is a disabled person for the purposes of the Disability Discrimination Act 1995; and

(b)   'disability' has the same meaning as in that Act.'

(8)   At any time before the coming into force of an order under paragraph (a)(i) or (b) of subsection (6), section 16 of the Chronically Sick and Disabled Persons Act 1970 (which extends the functions of the national advisory council) shall have effect as if after 'disabled persons' in each case there were inserted ', and persons who have had a disability,' and as if at the end of the section there were added—

'(2)   For the purposes of this section—

(a)   a person is a disabled person if he is a disabled person for the purposes of the Disability Discrimination Act 1995; and

(b)   'disability' has the same meaning as in that Act.'

61.   Amendment of Disabled Persons (Employment) Act 1944

(1)   Section 15 of the Disabled Persons (Employment) Act 1944 (which gives the Secretary of State power to make arrangements for the provision of supported employment) is amended as set out in subsections (2) to (5).

(2)   In subsection (1)—

(a)   for 'persons registered as handicapped by disablement' substitute 'disabled persons';

(b)   for 'their disablement' substitute 'their disability'; and

(c)   for 'are not subject to disablement' substitute 'do not have a disability'.

(3)   In subsection (2), for the words from 'any of one or more companies' to 'so required and prohibited' substitute 'any company, association or body'.

(4)   After subsection (2) insert—

'(2A)   The only kind of company which the Minister himself may form in exercising his powers under this section is a company which is—

(a)   required by its constitution to apply its profits, if any, or other income in promoting its objects; and

(b)   prohibited by its constitution from paying any dividend to its members.'

(5)   After subsection (5) insert—

'(5A)   For the purposes of this section—

(a)   a person is a disabled person if he is a disabled person for the purposes of the Disability Discrimination Act 1995; and

(b)   'disability' has the same meaning as in that Act.'

(6)   The provisions of section 16 (preference to be given under section 15 of that Act to ex-service men and women) shall become subsection (1) of that section and at the end insert—

'and whose disability is due to that service.

(2)   For the purposes of subsection (1) of this section, a disabled person's disability shall be treated as due to service of a particular kind only in such circumstances as may be prescribed.'

(7)   The following provisions of the Act of 1944 shall cease to have effect—

(a)   section 1 (definition of 'disabled person');

(b)   sections 6 to 8 (the register of disabled persons);

(c)   sections 9 to 11 (obligations on employers with substantial staffs to employ a quota of registered persons);

(d)   section 12 (the designated employment scheme for persons registered as handicapped by disablement);

    (e)   section 13 (interpretation of provisions repealed by this Act);

    (f)   section 14 (records to be kept by employers);

    (g)   section 19 (proceedings in relation to offences); and

    (h)   section 21 (application as respects place of employment, and nationality).

(8)   Any provision of subordinate legislation in which 'disabled person' is defined by reference to the Act of 1944 shall be construed as if that expression had the same meaning as in this Act.

(9)   Subsection (8) does not prevent the further amendment of any such provision by subordinate legislation.

62.   Restriction of publicity: industrial tribunals

(1)   This section applies to proceedings on a complaint under section 8 in which evidence of a personal nature is likely to be heard by the industrial tribunal hearing the complaint.

(2)   The power of the Secretary of State to make regulations with respect to the procedure of industrial tribunals includes power to make provision in relation to proceedings to which this section applies for—

    (a)   enabling an industrial tribunal, on the application of the complainant or of its own motion, to make a restricted reporting order having effect (if not revoked earlier) until the promulgation of the tribunal's decision; and

    (b)   where a restricted reporting order is made in relation to a complaint which is being dealt with by the tribunal together with any other proceedings, enabling the tribunal to direct that the order is to apply also in relation to those other proceedings or such part of them as the tribunal may direct.

(3)   If any identifying matter is published or included in a relevant programme in contravention of a restricted reporting order—

    (a)   in the case of publication in a newspaper or periodical, any proprietor, any editor and any publisher of the newspaper or periodical,

    (b)   in the case of publication in any other form, the person publishing the matter, and

    (c)   in the case of matter included in a relevant programme—

        (i)   any body corporate engaged in providing the service in which the programme is included, and

        (ii)   any person having functions in relation to the programme corresponding to those of an editor of a newspaper,

shall be guilty of an offence and liable on summary conviction to a fine not exceeding level 5 on the standard scale.

(4)   Where a person is charged with an offence under subsection (3), it is a defence to prove that at the time of the alleged offence—

    (a)   he was not aware, and

    (b)   he neither suspected nor had reason to suspect,

that the publication or programme in question was of, or included, the matter in question.

(5)   Where an offence under subsection (3) committed by a body corporate is proved to have been committed with the consent or connivance of, or to be attributable to any neglect on the part of—

    (a)   a director, manager, secretary or other similar officer of the body corporate, or

(b)   a person purporting to act in any such capacity,

he as well as the body corporate is guilty of the offence and liable to be proceeded against and punished accordingly.

(6)   In relation to a body corporate whose affairs are managed by its members 'director', in subsection (5), means a member of the body corporate.

(7)   In this section—

'evidence of a personal nature' means any evidence of a medical, or other intimate, nature which might reasonably be assumed to be likely to cause significant embarrassment to the complainant if reported;

'identifying matter' means any matter likely to lead members of the public to identify the complainant or such other persons (if any) as may be named in the order;

'promulgation' has such meaning as may be prescribed by the regulations;

'relevant programme' means a programme included in a programme service, within the meaning of the Broadcasting Act 1990;

'restricted reporting order' means an order—

(a)   made in exercise of the power conferred by regulations made by virtue of this section; and

(b)   prohibiting the publication in Great Britain of identifying matter in a written publication available to the public or its inclusion in a relevant programme for reception in Great Britain; and

'written publication' includes a film, a soundtrack and any other record in permanent form but does not include an indictment or other document prepared for use in particular legal proceedings.

63.   Restriction of publicity: Employment Appeal Tribunal

(1)   This section applies to proceedings—

(a)   on an appeal against a decision of an industrial tribunal to make, or not to make, a restricted reporting order, or

(b)   on an appeal against any interlocutory decision of an industrial tribunal in proceedings in which the industrial tribunal has made a restricted reporting order which it has not revoked.

(2)   The power of the Lord Chancellor to make rules with respect to the procedure of the Employment Appeal Tribunal includes power to make provision in relation to proceedings to which this section applies for—

(a)   enabling the Tribunal, on the application of the complainant or of its own motion, to make a restricted reporting order having effect (if not revoked earlier) until the promulgation of the Tribunal's decision; and

(b)   where a restricted reporting order is made in relation to an appeal which is being dealt with by the Tribunal together with any other proceedings, enabling the Tribunal to direct that the order is to apply also in relation to those other proceedings or such part of them as the Tribunal may direct.

(3)   Subsections (3) to (6) of section 62 apply in relation to a restricted reporting order made by the Tribunal as they apply in relation to one made by an industrial tribunal.

(4)   In subsection (1), 'restricted reporting order' means an order which is a restricted reporting order for the purposes of section 62.

(5)   In subsection (2), 'restricted reporting order' means an order—

(a) made in exercise of the power conferred by rules made by virtue of this section; and

(b) prohibiting the publication in Great Britain of identifying matter in a written publication available to the public or its inclusion in a relevant programme for reception in Great Britain.

(6) In this section—

'complainant' means the person who made the complaint to which the proceedings before the Tribunal relate;

'identifying matter', 'written publication' and 'relevant programme' have the same meaning as in section 62; and

'promulgation' has such meaning as may be prescribed by the rules.

64. Application to Crown etc.

(1) This Act applies—

(a) to an act done by or for purposes of a Minister of the Crown or government department, or

(b) to an act done on behalf of the Crown by a statutory body, or a person holding a statutory office,

as it applies to an act done by a private person.

(2) Subject to subsection (5), Part II applies to service—

(a) for purposes of a Minister of the Crown or government department, other than service of a person holding a statutory office, or

(b) on behalf of the Crown for purposes of a person holding a statutory office or purposes of a statutory body,

as it applies to employment by a private person.

(3) The provisions of Parts II to IV of the 1947 Act apply to proceedings against the Crown under this Act as they apply to Crown proceedings in England and Wales; but section 20 of that Act (removal of proceedings from county court to High Court) does not apply.

(4) The provisions of Part V of the 1947 Act apply to proceedings against the Crown under this Act as they apply to proceedings in Scotland which by virtue of that Part are treated as civil proceedings by or against the Crown; but the proviso to section 44 of that Act (removal of proceedings from the sheriff court to the Court of Session) does not apply.

(5) Part II does not apply to service—

(a) as a member of the Ministry of Defence Police, the British Transport Police, the Royal Parks Constabulary or the United Kingdom Atomic Energy Authority Constabulary;

(b) as a prison officer; or

(c) for purposes of a Minister of the Crown or government department having functions with respect to defence as a person who is or may be required by his terms of service to engage in fire fighting.

(6) Part II does not apply to service as a member of a fire brigade who is or may be required by his terms of service to engage in fire fighting

(7) It is hereby declared (for the avoidance of doubt) that Part II does not apply to service in any of the naval, military or air forces of the Crown.

(8) In this section—

'the 1947 Act' means the Crown Proceedings Act 1947;

'British Transport Police' means the constables appointed, or deemed to have been appointed, under section 53 of the British Transport Commission Act 1949;

'Crown proceedings' means proceedings which, by virtue of section 23 of the 1947 Act, are treated for the purposes of Part II of that Act as civil proceedings by or against the Crown;

'fire brigade' means a fire brigade maintained in pursuance of the Fire Services Act 1947;

'Ministry of Defence Police' means the force established under section 1 of the Ministry of Defence Police Act 1987;

'prison officer' means a person who is a prison officer within the meaning of section 127 of the Criminal Justice and Public Order Act 1994, apart from those who are custody officers within the meaning of Part I of that Act;

'Royal Parks Constabulary' means the park constables appointed under the Parks Regulation Act 1872;

'service for purposes of a Minister of the Crown or government department' does not include service in any office for the time being mentioned in Schedule 2 (Ministerial offices) to the House of Commons Disqualification Act 1975;

'statutory body' means a body set up by or under an enactment;

'statutory office' means an office so set up; and

'United Kingdom Atomic Energy Authority Constabulary' means the special constables appointed under section 3 of the Special Constables Act 1923 on the nomination of the United Kingdom Atomic Authority.

65. Application to Parliament

(1)   This Act applies to an act done by or for purposes of the House of Lords or the House of Commons as it applies to an act done by a private person.

(2)   For the purposes of the application of Part II in relation to the House of Commons, the Corporate Officer of the House shall be treated as the employer of a person who is (or would be) a relevant member of the House of Commons staff for the purposes of section 139 of the Employment Protection (Consolidation) Act 1978.

(3)   Except as provided in subsection (4), for the purposes of the application of sections 19 to 21, the provider of services is—

(a)   as respects the House of Lords, the Corporate Officer of that House; and

(b)   as respects the House of Commons, the Corporate Officer of that House.

(4)   Where the service in question is access to and use of any place in the Palace of Westminster which members of the public are permitted to enter, the Corporate Officers of both Houses jointly are the provider of that service.

(5)   Nothing in any rule of law or the law or practice of Parliament prevents proceedings being instituted before an industrial tribunal under Part II or before any court under Part III.

66. Government appointments outside Part II

(1)   Subject to regulations under subsection (3), this section applies to any appointment made by a Minister of the Crown or government department to an office or post where Part II does not apply in relation to the appointment.

(2)   In making the appointment, and in making arrangements for determining to whom the office or post should be offered, the Minister of the Crown or government department shall not act in a way which would contravene Part II if he or the department were the employer for the purposes of this Act.

(3)   Regulations may provide for this section not to apply to such appointments as may be prescribed.

67. Regulations and orders

(1)   Any power under this Act to make regulations or orders shall be exercisable by statutory instrument.

(2)   Any such power may be exercised to make different provision for different cases, including different provision for different areas of localities.

(3)   Any such power includes power—

(a)   to make such incidental, supplemental, consequential or transitional provision as appears to the Secretary of State to be expedient; and

(b)   to provide for a person to exercise a discretion in dealing with any matter.

(4)   No order shall be made under section 50(3) unless a draft of the statutory instrument containing the order has been laid before Parliament and approved by a resolution of each House.

(5)   Any other statutory instrument made under this Act, other than one made under section 3(9), 52(8), 54(6), or 70(3), shall be subject to annulment in pursuance of a resolution of either House of Parliament.

(6)   Subsection (1) does not require an order under section 43 which applies only to a specified vehicle, or to vehicles of a specified person, to be made by statutory instrument but such an order shall be as capable of being amended or revoked as an order which is made by statutory instrument.

(7)   Nothing in section 34(4), 40(6) or 46(5) affects the powers conferred by subsections (2) and (3).

68. Interpretation

(1)   In this Act—

'accessibility certificate' means a certificate issued under section 41(1)(a);

'act' includes a deliberate omission;

'approval certificate' means a certificate issued under section 42(4);

'benefits', in Part II, has the meaning given in section 4(4);

'conciliaton officer' means a person designated under section 211 of the Trade Union and Labour Relations (Consolidation) Act 1992;

'employment' means, subject to any prescribed provision, employment under a contract of service or of apprenticeship or a contract personally to do any work, and related expressions are to be construed accordingly;

'employment at an establishment in Great Britain' is to be construed in accordance with subsections (2) to (5);

'enactment' includes subordinate legislation and any Order in Council;

'licensing authority' means—

(a)   in relation to the area to which the Metropolitan Public Carriage Act 1869 applies, the Secretary of State or the holder of any office for the time being designated by the Secretary of State; or

(b)   in relation to any other area in England and Wales, the authority responsible for licensing taxis in that area;

'mental impairment' does not have the same meaning as in the Mental Health Act 1983 or the Mental Health (Scotland) Act 1984 but the fact that an impairment would be a mental impairment for the purposes of either of those Acts does not prevent it from being a mental impairment for the purposes of this Act;

'Minister of the Crown' includes the Treasury;

'occupational pension scheme' has the same meaning as in the Pension Schemes Act 1993;

'premises' includes land of any description;

'prescribed' means prescribed by regulations;

'profession' includes any vocation or occupation;

'provider of services' has the meaning given in section 19(2)(b);

'public service vehicle' and 'regulated public service vehicle' have the meaning given in section 40;

'PSV accessibility regulations' means regulations made under section 40(1);

'rail vehicle' and 'regulated rail vehicle' have the meaning given in section 46;

'rail vehicle accessibility regulations' means regulations made under section 46(1);

'regulations' means regulations made by the Secretary of State;

'section 6 duty' means any duty imposed by or under section 6;

'section 15 duty' means any duty imposed by or under section 15;

'section 21 duty' means any duty imposed by or under section 21;

'subordinate legislation' has the same meaning as in section 21 of the Interpretation Act 1978;

'taxi' and 'regulated taxi' have the meaning given in section 32;

'taxi accessibility regulations' means regulations made under section 32(1);

'trade' includes any business;

'trade organisation' has the meaning given in section 13;

'vehicle examiner' means an examiner appointed under section 66A of the Road Traffic Act 1988.

(2)   Where an employee does his work wholly or mainly outside Great Britain, his employment is not to be treated as being work at an establishment in Great Britain even if he does some of his work at such an establishment.

(3)   Except in prescribed cases, employment on board a ship, aircraft or hovercraft is to be regarded as not being employment at an establishment in Great Britain.

(4)   Employment of a prescribed kind, or in prescribed circumstances, is to be regarded as not being employment at an establishment in Great Britain.

(5)   Where work is not done at an establishment it shall be treated as done—

(a)   at the establishment from which it is done; or

(b)   where it is not done from any establishment, at the establishment with which it has the closest connection.

69.   Financial provisions

There shall be paid out of money provided by Parliament—

(a)   any expenditure incurred by a Minister of the Crown under this Act;

(b)   any increase attributable to this Act in the sums payable out of money so provided under or by virtue of any other enactment.

70.   Short title, commencement, extent etc.

(1)   This Act may be cited as the Disability Discrimination Act 1995.

(2)   This section (apart from subsections (4), (5) and (7)) comes into force on the passing of this Act.

(3)   The other provisions of this Act come into force on such day as the Secretary of State may by order appoint and different days may be appointed for different purposes.

(4)   Schedule 6 makes consequential amendments.

(5)   The repeals set out in Schedule 7 shall have effect.

(6)   This Act extends to Northern Ireland, but in their application to Northern Ireland the provisions of this Act mentioned in Schedule 8 shall have effect subject to the modifications set out in that Schedule.

(7)   In Part II of Schedule 1 to the House of Commons Disqualification Act 1975 and in Part II of Schedule 1 to the Northern Ireland Assembly Disqualification Act 1975 (bodies whose members are disqualified) in each case insert at the appropriate places—

'The National Disability Council.'

'The Northern Ireland Disability Council.'

(8)   Consultations which are required by any provision of this Act to be held by the Secretary of State may be held by him before the coming into force of that provision.

SCHEDULES

Section 1(1)   SCHEDULE 1
                    PROVISIONS SUPPLEMENTING SECTION 1

Impairment

1.—(1)   'Mental impairment' includes an impairment resulting from or consisting of a mental illness only if the illness is a clinically well-recognised illness.

(2)   Regulations may make provision, for the purposes of this Act—

(a)   for conditions of a prescribed description to be treated as amounting to impairments;

(b)   for conditions of a prescribed description to be treated as not amounting to impairments.

(3)   Regulations made under sub-paragraph (2) may make provision as to the meaning of 'condition' for the purposes of those regulations.

Long-term effects

2.—(1)   The effect of an impairment is a long-term effect if—

(a)   it has lasted at least 12 months;

(b)   the period for which it lasts is likely to be at least 12 months; or

(c)   it is likely to last for the rest of the life of the person affected.

(2)   Where an impairment ceases to have a substantial adverse effect on a person's ability to carry out normal day-to-day activities, it is to be treated as continuing to have that effect if that effect is likely to recur.

(3)   For the purposes of sub-paragraph (2), the likelihood of an effect recurring shall be disregarded in prescribed circumstances.

(4)   Regulations may prescribe circumstances in which, for the purposes of this Act—

(a)   an effect which would not otherwise be a long-term effect is to be treated as such an effect; or

(b)   an effect which would otherwise be a long-term effect is to be treated as not being such an effect.

Severe disfigurement

3.—(1) An impairment which consists of a severe disfigurement is to be treated as having a substantial adverse effect on the ability of the person concerned to carry out normal day-to-day activities.

(2) Regulations may provide that in prescribed circumstances a severe disfigurement is not to be treated as having that effect.

(3) Regulations under sub-paragraph (2) may, in particular, make provision with respect to deliberately acquired disfigurements.

Normal day-to-day activities

4.—(1) An impairment is to be taken to affect the ability of the person concerned to carry out normal day-to-day activities only if it affects one of the following—

  (a) mobility;
  (b) manual dexterity;
  (c) physical co-ordination;
  (d) continence;
  (e) ability to lift, carry or otherwise move everyday objects;
  (f) speech, hearing or eyesight;
  (g) memory or ability to concentrate, learn or understand; or
  (h) perception of the risk of physical danger.

(2) Regulations may prescribe—

  (a) circumstances in which an impairment which does not have an effect falling within sub-paragraph (1) is to be taken to affect the ability of the person concerned to carry out normal day-to-day activities;

  (b) circumstances in which an impairment which has an effect falling within sub-paragraph (1) is to be taken not to affect the ability of the person concerned to carry out normal day to day activities.

Substantial adverse effects

5. Regulations may make provision for the purposes of this Act—

  (a) for an effect of a prescribed kind on the ability of a person to carry out normal day-to-day activities to be treated as a substantial adverse effect;

  (b) for an effect of a prescribed kind on the ability of a person to carry out normal day-to-day activities to be treated as not being substantial adverse effect.

Effect of medical treatment

6.—(1) An impairment which would be likely to have a substantial adverse effect on the ability of the person concerned to carry out normal day-to-day activities, but for the fact that measures are being taken to treat or correct it, is to be treated as having that effect.

(2) In sub-paragraph (1) 'measures' includes, in particular, medical treatment and the use of a prosthesis or other aid.

(3) Sub-paragraph (1) does not apply—

  (a) in relation to the impairment of a person's sight, to the extent that the impairment is, in his case, correctable by spectacles or contact lenses or in such other ways as may be prescribed; or

  (b) in relation to such other impairments as may be prescribed, in such circumstances as may be prescribed.

Persons deemed to be disabled

7.—(1)   Sub-paragraph (2) applies to any person whose name is, both on 12th January 1995 and on the date when this paragraph comes into force, in the register of disabled persons maintained under section 6 of the Disabled Persons (Employment) Act 1944.

(2)   That person is to be deemed—

(a)   during the initial period, to have a disability, and hence to be a disabled person; and

(b)   afterwards, to have had a disability and hence to have been a disabled person during that period.

(3)   A certificate of registration shall be conclusive evidence, in relation to the person with respect to whom it was issued, of the matters certified.

(4)   Unless the contrary is shown, any document purporting to be a certificate of registration shall be taken to be such a certificate and to have been validly issued.

(5)   Regulations may provide for prescribed descriptions of person to be deemed to have disabilities, and hence to be disabled persons, for the purposes of this Act.

(6)   Regulations may prescribe circumstances in which a person who has been deemed to be a disabled person by the provisions of sub-paragraph (1) or regulations made under sub-paragraph (5) is to be treated as no longer being deemed to be such a person.

(7)   In this paragraph—

'certificate of registration' means a certificate issued under regulations made under section 6 of the Act of 1944; and

'initial period' means the period of three years beginning with the date on which this paragraph comes into force.

Progressive conditions

8.—(1)   Where—

(a)   a person has a progressive condition (such as cancer, multiple sclerosis or muscular dystrophy or infection by the human immunodeficiency virus),

(b)   as a result of that condition, he has an impairment which has (or had) an effect on his ability to carry out normal day-to-day activities, but

(c)   that effect is not (or was not) a substantial adverse effect,

he shall be taken to have an impairment which has such a substantial adverse effect if the condition is likely to result in his having such an impairment.

(2)   Regulations may make provision, for the purposes of this paragraph—

(a)   for conditions of a prescribed description to be treated as being progressive;

(b)   for conditions of a prescribed description to be treated as not being progressive.

Section 2(2)   SCHEDULE 2
                         PAST DISABILITIES

1.   The modifications referred to in section 2 are as follows.

2.   References in Parts II and III to a disabled person are to be read as references to a person who has had a disability.

3.   In section 6(1), after 'not disabled' insert 'and who have not had a disability'.

4.   In section 6(6), for 'has' substituted 'has had'.

5.   For paragraph 2(1) to (3) of Schedule 1, substitute—

'(1)   The effect of an impairment is a long-term effect if it has lasted for at least 12 months.

(2)   Where an impairment ceases to have a substantial adverse effect on a person's ability to carry out normal day-to-day activities, it is to be treated as continuing to have that effect if that effect recurs.

(3)   For the purposes of sub-paragraph (2), the recurrence of an effect shall be disregarded in prescribed circumstances.'

Sections 8(8) and 25(6)   SCHEDULE 3
ENFORCEMENT AND PROCEDURE
PART I   EMPLOYMENT

Conciliation

1.—(1)   Where a complaint is presented to an industrial tribunal under section 8 and a copy of it is sent to a conciliation officer, he shall—

(a)   if requested to do so by the complainant and respondent, or

(b)   if he considers that he has a reasonable prospect of success,

try to promote a settlement of the complaint without its being determined by an industrial tribunal.

(2)   Where a person is contemplating presenting such a complaint, a conciliation officer shall, if asked to do so by the potential complainant or potential respondent, try to promote a settlement.

(3)   The conciliation officer shall, where appropriate, have regard to the desirability of encouraging the use of other procedures available for the settlement of grievances.

(4)   Anything communicated to a conciliation officer in a case in which he is acting under this paragraph shall not be admissible in evidence in any proceedings before an industrial tribual except with the consent of the person who communicated it.

Restriction on proceedings for breach of Part II

2.—(1)   Except as provided by section 8, no civil or crminal proceedings may be brought against any person in respect of an act merely because the act is unlawful under Part II.

(2)   Sub-paragraph (1) does not prevent the making of an application for judicial review.

Period within which proceedings must be brought

3.—(1)   An industrial tribunal shall not consider a complaint under section 8 unless it is presented before the end of the period of three months beginning when the act complained of was done.

(2)   A tribunal may consider any such complaint which is out of time if, in all the circumstances of the case, it considers that it is just and equitable to do so.

(3)   For the purposes of sub-paragraph (1)—

(a)   where an unlawful act of discrimination is attributable to a term in a contract, that act is to be treated as extending throughout the duration of the contract;

(b)   any act extending over a period shall be treated as done at the end of that period; and

(c)   a deliberate omission shall be treated as done when the person in question decided upon it.

(4)   In the absence of evidence establishing the contrary, a person shall be taken for the purposes of this paragraph to decide upon an omission—

(a)   when he does an act inconsistent with doing the omitted act; or

(b)   if he has done no such inconsistent act, when the period expires within which he might reasonably have been expected to do the omitted act if it was to be done.

Evidence

4.—(1)   In any proceedings under section 8, a certificate signed by or on behalf of a Minister of the Crown and certifying—

(a)   that any conditions or requirements specified in the certificate were imposed by a Minister of the Crown and were in operation at a time or throughout a time so specified, or

(b)   that an act specified in the certificate was done for the purpose of safeguarding national security,
shall be conclusive evidence of the matters certified.

(2)   A document purporting to be such a certificate shall be received in evidence and, unless the contrary is proved, be deemed to be such a certificate.

PART II   DISCRIMINATION IN OTHER AREAS

Restriction on proceedings for breach of Part III

5.—(1)   Except as provided by section 25 no civil or criminal proceedings may be brought against any person in respect of an act merely because the act is unlawful under Part III.

(2)   Sub-paragraph (1) does not prevent the making of an application for judicial review.

Period within which proceedings must be brought

6.—(1)   A county court or a sheriff court shall not consider a claim under section 25 unless proceedings in respect of the claim are instituted before the end of the period of six months beginning when the act complained of was done.

(2)   Where, in relation to proceedings or prospective proceedings under section 25, a person appointed in connection with arrangements under section 28 is approached befor the end of the period of six months mentioned in sub-paragraph (1), the period allowed by that sub-paragraph shall be extended by two months.

(3)   A court may consider any claim under section 25 which is out of time if, in all the circumstances of the case, it considers that it is just and equitable to do so.

(4)   For the purposes of sub-paragraph (1)—

(a)   where an unlawful act of discrimination is attributable to a term in a contract, that act is to be treated as extending throughout the duration of the contract;

(b)   any act extending over a period shall be treated as done at the end of that period; and

(c)   a deliberate omission shall be treated as done when the person in question decided upon it.

(5)   In the absence of evidence establishing the contrary, a person shall be taken for the purposes of this paragraph to decide upon an omission—

(a)   when he does an act inconsistent with doing the omitted act; or

(b)   if he has done no such inconsistent act, when the period expires within which he might reasonably have been expected to do the omitted act if it was to be done.

Compensation for injury to feelings

7.   In any proceedings under section 25, the amount of any damage awarded as compensation for injury to feeling shall not exceed the prescribed amount.

Evidence

8.—(1)   In any proceedings under section 25, a certificate signed by or on behalf of a Minister of the Crown and certifying—

(a)   that any conditions or requirements specified in the certificate were imposed by a Minister of the Crown and were in operation at a time or throughout a time so specified, or

(b)   that an act specified in the certificate was done for the purpose of safeguarding national security,

shall be conclusive evidence of the matters certified.

(2)   A document purporting to be such a certificate shall be received in evidence and, unless the contrary is proved, be deemed to be such a certificate.

Sections 16(5) and 27(5)   SCHEDULE 4
PREMISES OCCUPIED UNDER LEASES
PART I   OCCUPATION BY EMPLOYER OR TRADE ORGANISATION

Failure to obtain consent to alteration

1.   If any question arises as to whether the occupier has failed to comply with the section 6 or section 15 duty, by failing to make a particular alteration to the premises, any constraint attributable to the fact that he occupies the premises under a lease is to be ignored unless he has applied to the lessor in writing for consent to the making of the alteration.

Joining lessors in proceedings under section 8

2.—(1)   In any proceedings under section 8, in a case to which section 16 applies, the complainant or the occupier may ask the tribunal hearing the complaint to direct that the lessor be joined or sisted as a party to the proceedings.

(2)   The request shall be granted if it is made before the hearing of the complaint begins.

(3)   The tribunal may refuse the request if it is made after the hearing of the complaint begins.

(4)   The request may not be granted if it is made after the tribunal has determined the complaint.

(5)   Where a lessor has been so joined or sisted as a party to the proceedings, the tribunal may determine—

(a)   whether the lessor has—
  (i)   refused consent to the alteration, or
  (ii)   consented subject to one or more conditions, and
(b)   if so, whether the refusal or any of the conditions was unreasonable,

(6)   If, under sub-paragraph (5), the tribunal determines that the refusal or any of the conditions was unreasonable it may take one or more of the following steps—

(a)   make such declaration as it considers appropriate;
(b)   make an order authorising the occupier to make the alteration specified in the order;
(c)   order the lessor to pay compensation to the complainant.

(7)   An order under sub-paragraph (6)(b) may require the occupier to comply with conditions specified in the order.

(8)   Any step taken by the tribunal under sub-paragraph (6) may be in substitution for, or in addition to, any step taken by the tribunal under section 8(2).

(9)   If the tribunal orders the lessor to pay compensation it may not make an order under section 8(2) ordering the occupier to do so.

Regulations

3.   Regulations may make provision as to circumstances in which—
(a)   a lessor is to be taken, for the purposes of section 16 and this Part of this Schedule to have—
  (i)   withheld his consent;
  (ii)   withheld his consent unreasonably;
  (iii) acted reasonably in withholding his consent;
(b)   a condition subject to which a lessor has given his consent is to be taken to be reasonable;
(c)   a condition subject to which a lessor has given his consent is to be taken to be unreasonable.

Sub-leases etc.

4.   The Secretary of State may be regulations make provision supplementing, or modifying, the provision made by section 16 or any provision made by or under this Part of this Schedule in relation to cases where the occupier occupies premises under a sub-lease or sub-tenancy.

PART II   OCCUPATION BY PROVIDER OF SERVICES

Failure to obtain consent to alteration

5.   If any question arises as to whether the occupier has failed to comply with the section 21 duty, by failing to make a particular alteration to premises, any constraint attributable to the fact that he occupies the premises under a lease is to be ignored unless he has applied to the lessor in writing for consent to the making of the alteration.

Reference to court

6.—(1)   If the occupier has applied in writing to the lessor for consent to the alteration and—
(a)   that consent has been refused, or

(b)   the lessor has made his consent subject to one or more conditions,
the occupier or a disabled person who has an interest in the proposed alteration to the premises being made, may refer the matter to a county court or, in Scotland, to the sheriff.

(2)   In the following provisions of this Schedule 'court' includes 'sheriff'.

(3)   On such a reference the court shall determine whether the lessor's refusal was unreasonable or (as the case may be) whether the condition is, or any of the conditions are, unreasonable.

(4)   If the court determines—

(a)   that the lessor's refusal was unreasonable, or

(b)   that the condition is, or any of the conditions are, unreasonable,

it may make such declaration as it considers appropriate or an order authorising the occupier to make the alteration specified in the order.

(5)   An order under sub-paragraph (4) may require the occupier to comply with conditions specified in the order.

Joining lessors in proceedings under section 25

7.—(1)   In any proceedings on a claim under section 25, in a case to which this Part of this Schedule applies, the plaintiff, the pursuer or the occupier concerned may ask the court to direct that the lessor be joined or sisted as a party to the proceedings.

(2)   The request shall be granted if it is made before the hearing of the claim begins.

(3)   The court may refuse the request if it is made after the hearing of the claim begins.

(4)   The request may not be granted if it is made after the court has determined the claim.

(5)   Where a lessor has been so joined or sisted as a party to the proceedings, the court may determine—

(a)   whether the lessor has—

(i)   refused consent to the alteration, or

(ii)   consented subject to one or more conditions, and

(b)   if so, whether the refusal or any of the conditions was unreasonable.

(6)   If, under sub-paragraph (5), the court determines that the refusal or any of the conditions was unreasonable it may take one or more of the following steps—

(a)   make such declaration as it considers appropriate;

(b)   make an order authorising the occupier to make the alteration specified in the order;

(c)   order the lessor to pay compensation to the complainant.

(7)   An order under sub-paragraph (6)(b) may require the occupier to comply with conditions specified in the order.

(8)   If the court orders the lessor to pay compensation it may not order the occupier to do so.

Regulations

8.   Regulations may make provision as to circumstances in which—

(a)   a lessor is to be taken, for the purposes of section 27 and this Part of this Schedule to have—

(i)   withheld his consent;

      (ii)   withheld his consent unreasonably;

      (iii)   acted reasonably in withholding his consent;

  (b)   a condition subject to which a lessor has given his consent is to be taken to be reasonable;

  (c)   a condition subject to which a lessor has given his consent is to be taken to be unreasonable.

Sub-leases etc.

9.   The Secretary of State may be regulations make provision supplementing, or modifying, the provision made by section 27 or any provision made by or under this Part of this Schedule in relation to cases where the occupier occupies premises under a sub-lease or sub-tenancy.

Section 50(8)   SCHEDULE 5
                 THE NATIONAL DISABILITY COUNCIL

Status

1.—(1)   The Council shall be a body corporate.

(2)   The Council is not the servant or agent of the Crown and does not enjoy any status, immunity or privilege of the Crown.

Procedure

2.   The Council has power to regulate its own procedure (including power to determine its quorum).

Membership

3.—(1)   The Council shall consist of at least 10, but not more than 20 members.

(2)   In this Schedule 'member', except in sub-paragraph (5)(b), means a member of the Council.

(3)   Each member shall be appointed by the Secretary of State.

(4)   The Secretary of State shall appoint one member to be chairman of the Council and another member to be its deputy chairman.

(5)   The members shall be appointed from among persons who, in the opinion of the Secretary of State—

  (a)   have knowledge or experience of the needs of disabled persons or the needs of a particular group or particular groups, of disabled persons;

  (b)   have knowledge or experience of the needs of persons who have had a disability or the needs of a particular group, or particular groups, of such persons; or

  (c)   are members of, or otherwise represent, professional bodies or bodies which represent industry or other business interests.

(6)   Before appointing any member, the Secretary of State shall consult such persons as he considers appropriate.

(7)   In exercising his powers of appointment, the Secretary of State shall try to secure that at all times at least half the membership of the Council consists of disabled persons, persons who have had a disability or the parents or guardians of disabled persons.

Terms of office of members

4.—(1)   Each member shall be appointed for a term which does not exceed five years but shall otherwise hold and vacate his office in accordance with the terms of his appointment.

(2)   A person shall not be prevented from being appointed as a member merely because he has previously been a member.

(3)   Any member may at any time resign his office by written notice given to the Secretary of State.

(4)   Regulations may make provision for the Secretary of State to remove a member from his office in such circumstances as may be prescribed.

Remuneration

5.—(1)   The Secretary of State may pay such remuneration or expenses to any member as he considers appropriate.

(2)   The approval of the Treasury is required for any payment made under this paragraph.

Staff

6.   The Secretary of State shall provide the Council with such staff as he considers appropriate.

Supplementary regulation-making power

7.   The Secretary of State may by regulations make provision—

(a)   as to the provision of information to the Council by the Secretary of State;

(b)   as to the commissioning by the Secretary of State of research to be undertaken on behalf of Council;

(c)   as to the circumstances in which and conditions subject to which the Council may appoint any person as an adviser;

(d)   as to the payment by the Secretary of State, with the approval of the Treasury, of expenses incurred by the Council.

Annual report

8.—(1)   As soon as is practicable after the end of each financial year, the Council shall report to the Secretary of State on its activities during the financial year to which the report relates.

(2)   The Secretary of State shall lay a copy of every annual report of the Council before each House of Parliament and shall arrange for such further publication of the report as he considers appropriate.

Section 70(4)   SCHEDULE 6
                    CONSEQUENTIAL AMENDMENTS

Employment and Training Act 1973 (c. 50)

1.   In section 12(1) of the Employment and Training Act 1973 (duty of Secretary of State to give preference to ex-service men and women in exercising certain powers in respect of disabled persons)—

(a)   for 'persons registered as handicapped by disablement' substitute 'disabled persons'; and

(b)   for the words after 'disabled person' substitute 'has the same meaning as in the Disability Discrimination Act 1995'.

Employment Protection (Consolidation) Act 1978 (c. 44)

2.   In section 136(1) of the Employment Protection (Consolidation) Act 1978 (appeals to Employment Appeal Tribunal), at the end insert—
     '(ff)   the Disability Discrimination Act 1995'.

3.   In paragraph 20 of Schedule 13 to that Act (reinstatement or re-engagement of dismissed employees), in sub-paragraph (3)—
     (a)   in the definition of 'relevant complaint or dismissal', omit 'or' and at the end insert 'or a complaint under section 8 of the Disability Discrimination Act 1995 arising out of a dismissal';
     (b)   in the definition of 'relevant conciliation powers', omit 'or' and at the end insert 'or paragraph 1 of Schedule 3 to the Disability Discrimination Act 1995'; and
     (c)   in the definition of 'relevant compromise contract' for 'or section' substitute 'section' and at the end insert 'or section 9(2) of the Disability Discrimination Act 1995'.

Companies Act 1985 (c. 6)

4.   In paragraph 9 of Schedule 7 to the Companies Act 1985 (disclosure in directors' report of company policy in relation to disabled persons), in the definition of 'disabled person' in sub-paragraph (4)(b), for 'Disabled Persons (Employment) Act 1944' substitute 'Disability Discrimination Act 1995'.

Local Government and Housing Act 1989 (c. 42)

5.   In section 7 of the Local Government and Housing Act 1989 (all staff of a local authority etc. to be appointed on merit), in subsection (2)—
     (a)   paragraph (a) shall be omitted;
     (b)   the word 'and' at the end of paragraph (d) shall be omitted; and
     (c)   after paragraph (e) insert—
     '; and
         (f)   sections 5 and 6 of the Disability Discrimination Act 1995 (meaning of discrimination and duty to make adjustments).'

Enterprise and New Towns (Scotland) Act 1990 (c. 35)

6.   In section 16 of the Enterprise and New Towns (Scotland) Act 1990 (duty of certain Scottish bodies to give preference to ex-service men and women in exercising powers to select disabled persons for training), in subsection (2), for 'said Act of 1944' substitute 'Disability Discrimination Act 1995'.

SCHEDULE 7
REPEALS

Chapter	Short title	Extent of repeal
7 & 8 Geo. 6 c. 10.	The Disabled Persons (Employment) Act 1944.	Section 1. Sections 6 to 14. Section 19. Section 21. Section 22(4).
6 & 7 Eliz. 2 c. 33.	The Disabled Persons (Employment) Act 1958.	Section 2.
1970 c. 44.	The Chronically Sick and Disabled Persons Act 1970.	Section 16.
1978 c. 44.	The Employment Protection (Consolidation) Act 1978.	In Schedule 13, in paragraph 20(3), the word 'or' in the definitions of 'relevant complaint of dismissal' and 'relevant conciliation powers'.
1989 c. 42.	The Local Government and Housing Act 1989.	In section 7(2), paragraph (a) and the word 'and' at the end of paragraph (d).
1993 c. 62.	The Education Act 1993.	In section 161(5), the words from 'and in this subsection' to the end.

Section 70(6)   SCHEDULE 8
MODIFICATIONS OF THIS ACT IN ITS APPLICATION TO
NORTHERN IRELAND

1.   In its application to Northern Ireland this Act shall have effect subject to the following modifications.

2.—(1)   In section 3(1) for 'Secretary of State' substitute 'Department'.

(2)   In section 3 for subsections (4) to (12) substitute—

'(4)   In preparing a draft of any guidance, the Department shall consult such persons as it considers appropriate.

(5)   Where the Department proposes to issue any guidance, the Department shall publish a draft of it, consider any representations that are made to the Department about the draft and, if the Department thinks it appropriate, modify its proposals in the light of any of those representations.

(6)   If the Department decides to proceed with any proposed guidance, the Department shall lay a draft of it before the Assembly.

(7)   If, within the statutory period, the Assembly resolves not to approve the draft, the Department shall take no further steps in relation to the proposed guidance.

(8)   If no such resolution is made within the statutory period, the Department shall issue the guidance in the form of its draft.

(9)   The guidance shall come into force on such date as the Department may by order appoint.

(10)   Subsection (7) does not prevent a new draft of the proposed guidance being laid before the Assembly.

(11)   The Department may—

(a)   from time to time revise the whole or any part of any guidance and re-issue it;

(b)   by order revoke any guidance.

(12)   In this section—

'the Department' means the Department of Economic Development;

'guidance' means guidance issued by the Department under this section and includes guidance which has been revised and re-issued;

'statutory period' has the meaning assigned to it by section 41(2) of the Interpretation Act (Northern Ireland) 1954.'

3.   In section 4(6) for 'Great Britain' substitute 'Northern Ireland'.

4.—(1)   In section 7(2) for 'Secretary of State' substitute 'Department of Economic Development'.

(2)   In section 7(4) to (10) for 'Secretary of State' wherever it occurs substitute 'Department of Economic Development', for 'he' and 'him' wherever they occur substitute 'it' and for 'his' wherever it occurs substitute 'its'.

(3)   In section 7(9) for 'Parliament' substitute 'the Assembly'.

5.—(1)   In section 8(3) omit 'or (in Scotland) in reparation'.

(2)   In section 8(7) for 'paragraph 6A of Schedule 9 to the Employment Protection (Consolidation) Act 1978' substitute 'Article 61(3) of the Industrial Relations (Northern Ireland) Order 1976'.

6.—(1)   In section 9(2)(a) for 'a conciliation officer' substitute 'the Agency'.

(2)   In section 9(4) in the definition of 'qualified lawyer' for the words from 'means' to the end substitute 'means a barrister (whether in practice as such or employed to give legal advice) or a solicitor of the Supreme Court who holds a practising certificate'.

7.—(1)   In section 10(1)(b) omit 'or recognised body'.

(2)   In section 10(2)(b) for 'Secretary of State' substitute 'Department of Economic Development'.

(3)   In section 10(3) in the definition of 'charity' for '1993' substitute '(Northern Ireland) 1964', omit the definition of 'recognised body' and in the definition of 'supported employment' for 'Act 1944' substitute 'Act (Northern Ireland) 1945'.

(4)   In section 10(4) for 'England and Wales' where it twice occurs substitute 'Northern Ireland'.

(5)   Omit section 10(5).

8.—In section 12(5) for 'Great Britain' where it twice occurs substitute 'Northern Ireland'.

9.—(1)   In section 19(3)(g) for 'section 2 of the Employment and Training Act 1973' substitute 'sections 1 and 2 of the Employment and Training Act (Northern Ireland) 1950'.

(2)   In section 19(5) for paragraph (a) substitute—

'(a)   education which is funded, or secured, by a relevant body or provided at—

(i)   an establishment which is funded by such a body or by the Department of Education for Northern Ireland; or

(ii)   any other establishment which is a school within the meaning of the Education and Libraries (Northern Ireland) Order 1986;'.

(3)   For section 19(6) substitute—
    '(6)   In subsection (5) 'relevant body' means—
       (a)   an education and library board;
       (b)   a voluntary organisation; or
       (c)   a body of a prescribed kind.'.

10.   In section 20(7) for paragraphs (b) and (c) substitute '; or
    (b)   functions conferred by or under Part VIII of the Mental Health (Northern Ireland) Order 1986 are exercisable in relation to a disabled person's property or affairs.'.

11.   In section 22(4) and (6) omit 'or (in Scotland) the subject of'.

12.—(1)   In section 25(1) omit 'or (in Scotland) in reparation'.

(2)   In section 25(3) for 'England and Wales' substitute 'Northern Ireland'.

(3)   Omit section 25(4).

(4)   In section 25(5) omit the words from 'or' to the end.

13.   In section 26(3) omit 'or a sheriff court'.

14.—(1)   In section 28 for 'Secretary of State' wherever it occurs substitute 'Department of Health and Social Services'.

(2)   In section 28(3) and (4) for 'he' substitute 'it'.

(3)   In section 28(5) for 'Treasury' substitute 'Department of Finance and Personnel in Northern Ireland'.

15.   Omit sections 29, 30 and 31.

16.—(1)   In section 32(1) for 'Secretary of State' substitute 'Department of the Environment'.

(2)   In section 32(5) for the definition of 'taxi' substitute—
    ''taxi' means a vehicle which—
       (a)   is licensed under Article 61 of the Road Traffic (Northern Ireland) Order 1981 to stand or ply for hire; and
       (b)   seats not more than 8 passengers in addition to the driver'.

17.   In section 33, for 'Secretary of State', wherever it occurs, substitute 'Department of the Environment'.

18.   For section 34 substitute—

34.   'New licences conditional on compliance with accessibility taxi regulations

(1)   The Department of the Environment shall not grant a public service vehicle licence under Article 61 of the Road Traffic (Northern Ireland) Order 1981 for a taxi unless the vehicle conforms with those provisions of the taxi accessibility regulations with which it will be required to conform if licensed.

(2)   Subsection (1) does not apply if such a licence was in force with respect to the vehicle at any time during the period of 28 days immediately before the day on which the licence is granted.

(3)   The Department of the Environment may by order provide for subsection (2) to cease to have effect on such date as may be specified in the order.'.

19.   Omit section 35.

20.   In section 36(7) for 'licensing authority' substitute 'Department of the Environment'.

21.—(1)   In section 37(5) and (6) for 'licensing authority' substitute 'Department of the Environment'.

(2) In section 37(9) for 'Secretry of State' substitute 'Department of the Environment'.

22.—(1) In section 38(1) for 'a licensing authority' substitute 'the Department of the Environment'.

(2) In section 38(2) for 'licensing authority concerned' substitute 'Department of the Environment'.

(3) In section 38(3) for the words from 'the magistrates' court' to the end substitute 'a court of summary jurisdiction acting for the petty sessions district in which the aggrieved person resides'.

23. Omit section 39.

24.—(1) In section 40 for 'Secretary of State' wherever it occurs substitute 'Department of the Environment'.

(2) In section 40(5) for the definition of 'public service vehicle' substitute—
     ''public service vehicle' means a vehicle which—
          (a) seats more than 8 passengers in addition to the driver; and
          (b) is a public service vehicle for the purposes of the Road Traffic (Northern Ireland) Order 1981;'

(3) In section 40(7) for the words from 'the Disabled' to the end substitute 'such representative organisations as it thinks fit'.

25.—(1) In section 41(2) for 'Secretary of State' substitute 'Department of the Environment'.

(2) In section 41 for subsections (3) and (4) substitute—
     '(3) Any person who uses a regulated public service vehicle in contravention of this section is guilty of an offence and liable on summary conviction to a fine not exceeding level 4 on the standard scale.'.

26.—(1) In section 42 for 'Secretary of State' wherever it occurs substitute 'Department of the Environment'.

(2) In section 42(1) for 'he' substitute 'it'.

(3) In section 42(6) for 'his' substitute 'its'.

27. In section 43 for 'Secretary of State' wherever it occurs substitute 'Department of the Environment'.

28.—(1) In section 44 for 'Secretary of State' wherever it occurs substitute 'Department of the Environment'.

(2) In section 44(2) for 'him' substitute 'it'.

(3) In section 44(6) for 'he' substitute 'it' and for 'his' substitute 'its'.

29.—(1) In section 45 for 'Secretary of State' wherever it occurs substitute 'Department of the Environment'.

(2) In section 45(2) for 'him' substitute 'it' and at the end add 'of Northern Ireland'.

(3) In section 45(4) for 'he' substitute 'it'.

30.—(1) In section 46 for 'Secretary of State' wherever it occurs substitute 'Department of the Environment'.

(2) In section 46(6) in the definition of 'rail vehicle' for the words 'on any railway, tramway or prescribed system' substitute 'by rail'.

(3) Omit section 46(7).

(4) In section 46(11) for the words from 'the Disabled' to the end substitute 'such representative organisations as it thinks fit'.

31.—(1) In section 47 for 'Secretary of State' wherever it occurs substitute 'Department of the Environment'.

(2)   In section 47(3) for the words 'the Disabled Persons Transport Advisory Committee and such other persons as he' substitute 'such persons as it' and for 'he' substitute 'it'.

32.   Omit section 48(3).

33.—(1)   In the heading to Part VI of this Act and in section 50(1) for 'National Disability Council' substitute 'Northern Ireland Disability Council'.

(2)   In section 50(2) for 'the Secretary of State' in the first place where it occurs substitute 'a Northern Ireland Department' and in the other place where it occurs substitute 'that department'.

(3)   In section 50(3) for 'Secretary of State' substitute 'Department of Health and Social Services'.

(4)   In section 50(7) for 'the Secretary of State' substitute 'a Northern Ireland department' and after 'crown' insert 'or a Northern Ireland department'.

(5)   In section 50(9)(a) for sub-paragraphs (i) to (iv) substitute—

   '(i)   the Disabled Persons (Employment) Act (Northern Ireland) 1945;

   (ii)   the Contracts of Employment and Redundancy Payments Act (Northern Ireland) 1965;

   (iii)   the Employment and Training Act (Northern Ireland) 1950;

   (iv)   the Industrial Relations (Northern Ireland) Orders 1976; or.'

(6)   In section 50(10) for the words from 'time when' to the end substitute 'time when—

(a)   there are no committees in existence under section 17 of the Disabled Persons (Employment) Act (Northern Ireland) 1945; and

(b)   there is no person appointed to act generally under section 60(1) of this Act.'.

34.—(1)   In section 51(1) for 'the Secretary of State' substitute 'any Northern Ireland department' and for 'the Secretary of State's' substitute 'that department's'.

(2)   In section 51(2) for 'The Secretary of State' substitute 'A Northern Ireland department'.

(3)   In section 51(4) for 'a county court or a sheriff court' substitute 'or a county court'.

(4)   In section 51(6) for 'the Secretary of State' substitute 'a Northern Ireland department'.

35.   For section 52 substitute—

52.   'Further provisions about codes issued under section 51

(1)   In this section—

'proposal' means a proposal made by the Council to a Northern Ireland department under section 51;

'responsible department'—

(a)   in relation to a proposal, means the Northern Ireland department to which the proposal is made,

(b)   in relation to a code, means the Northern Ireland department by which the code is issued; and

'statutory period' has the meaning assigned to it by section 41(2) of the Interpretation Act (Northern Ireland) 1954.

(2)   In preparing any proposal, the Council shall consult—

(a)   such persons (if any) as the responsible department has specified in making its request to the Council; and

(b)   such other persons (if any) as the Council considers appropriate.

(3)   Before making any proposal the council shall publish a draft, consider any representations made to it about the draft and, if it thinks it appropriate, modify its proposal in the light of any of those representations.

(4)   Where the Council makes any proposal, the responsible department may—

(a)   approve it;

(b)   approve it subject to such modifications as that department thinks appropriate; or

(c)   refuse to approve it.

(5)   Where the responsible department approves any proposal (with or without modifications) that department shall prepare a draft of the proposed code and lay it before the Assembly.

(6)   If, within the statutory period, the Assembly resolves not to approve the draft, the responsible department shall take no further steps in relation to the proposed code.

(7)   If no such resolution is made within the statutory period, the responsible department shall issue the code in the form of its draft.

(8)   The code shall come into force on such date as the responsible department may appoint by order.

(9)   Subsection (6) does not prevent a new draft of the proposed code from being laid before the Assembly.

10   If the responsible department refuses to approve a proposal, that department shall give the Council a written statement of the department's reasons for not approving it.

(11)   The responsible department may by order revoke a code.'.

36.—(1)   In section 53 for 'Secretary of State' wherever it occurs substitute 'Department of Economic Development'.

(2)   In section 53(1) for 'he' substitute 'it'.

(3)   In section 53(5) for 'a county court or a sheriff court' substitute 'or a county court'.

37.   For section 54 substitute—

54.   'Further provisions about codes issued under section 53

(1)   In preparing a draft of any code under section 53, the Department shall consult such organisations representing the interests of employers or of disabled persons in, or seeking, employment as the Department considers appropriate.

(2)   Where the Department proposes to issue a code, the Department shall publish a draft of the code, consider any representations that are made to the Department about the draft and, if the Department thinks it appropriate, modify its proposals in the light of any of those representations.

(3)   If the Department decides to proceed with the code, the Department shall lay a draft of it before the Assembly.

(4)   If, within the statutory period, the Assembly resolves not to approve the draft, the Department shall take no further steps in relation to the proposed code.

(5)   If no such resolution is made within the statutory period, the Department shall issue the code in the form of its draft.

(6)   The code shall come into force on such date as the Department may appoint by order.

(7)   Subsection (4) does not prevent a new draft of the proposed code from being laid before the Assembly.

(8)   The Department may by order revoke a code.

(9)   In this section—

'the Department' means the Department of Economic Development; and

'statutory period' has the meaning assigned to it by section 41(2) of the Interpretation Act (Northern Ireland) 1954.'.

38.   In section 56(2) and (4) for 'Secretary of State' substitute 'Department of Economic Development'.

39.   In section 59(1) after 'Crown' where it twice occurs insert 'or a Northern Ireland department'.

40.—(1)   In section 60(1) to (3) for 'Secretary of State' wherever it occurs substitute 'Department of Economic Development' and for 'he' and 'him' wherever they occur substitute 'it'.

(2)   In section 60(4) for 'Treasury' substitute 'Department of Finance and Personnel in Northern Ireland'.

(3)   For section 60(6) substitute—

'(6)   The Department of Economic Development may by order repeal section 17 of, and Schedule 2 to, the Disabled Persons (Employment) Act (Northern Ireland) 1945 (district advisory committees).'

(4)   In section 60(7) omit 'paragraph (b) or', for '1944' substitute '1945' and omit 'in each case'.

(5)   In section 60, omit subsection (8).

41.   For section 61 substitute—

61.   'Amendments of Disabled Persons (Employment) Act (Northern Ireland) 1945

(1)   Section 15 of the Disabled Persons (Employment) Act (Northern Ireland) 1945 (which gives the Department of Economic Development power to make arrangements for the provision of supported employment) is amended as set out in subsections (2) to (5).

(2)   In subsection (1)—

(a)   for 'persons registered as handicapped by disablement' substitute 'disabled persons';

(b)   for 'their disablement' substitute 'their disability'; and

(c)   for 'are not subject to disablement' substitute 'do not have a disability'.

(3)   In subsection (2) for the words from 'any of one or more companies' to 'so required and prohibited' substitute 'any company, association or body'.

(4)   After subsection (2) insert—

'(2A)   The only kind of company which the Department itself may form in exercising its powers under this section is a company which is—

(a)   required by its constitution to apply its profits, if any, or other income in promoting its objects; and

(b)   prohibited by its constitution from paying any dividend to its members.'.

(5)   After subsection (5) insert—

'(5A)   For the purposes of this section—

(a)   a person is a disabled person if he is a disabled person for the purposes of the Disability Discrimination Act 1995; and

(b)   'disability' has the same meaning as in that Act.'.

(6)   The provisions of section 16 of the Act of 1945 (preference to be given under section 15 of that Act to ex-service men and women) shall become subsection (1) of that section and at the end insert—

'and whose disability is due to that service.

(2)   For the purposes of subsection (1) of this section, a disabled person's disability shall be treated as due to service of a particular kind only in such circumstances as may be prescribed.'

(7)   The following provisions of the Act of 1945 shall cease to have effect—

(a)   section 1 (definition of 'disabled person');

(b)   sections 2 to 4 (training for disabled persons);

(c)   sections 6 to 8 (the register of disabled persons);

(d)   sections 9 to 11 (obligations on employers with substantial staffs to employ quota of registered persons);

(e)   section 12 (the designated employment scheme for persons registered as handicapped by disablement);

(f)   section 13 (interpretation of provisions repealed by this Act);

(g)   section 14 (records to be kept by employer);

(h)   section 19 (proceedings in relation to offences);

(j)   sections 21 and 22 (supplementary).

(8)   Any statutory provision in which 'disabled person' is defined by reference to the Act of 1945 shall be construed as if that expression had the same meaning as in this Act.'.

42.—(1)   In section 62(2) for 'Secretary of State' substitute 'Department of Economic Development'.

(2)   In section 62(7) for 'Great Britain' where it twice occurs substitute 'Northern Ireland'.

43.   Omit section 63.

44.—(1)   In section 64(3) for 'England and Wales' substitute 'Northern Ireland'.

(2)   Omit section 64(4);

(3)   In section 64(5)(a) omit the words from ', the British' to the end.

(4)   In section 64(8)—

(a)   omit the definitions of 'British Transport Police', 'Royal Parks Constabulary' and 'United Kingdom Atomic Energy Authority Constabulary';

(b)   in the definition of 'the 1947 Act' at the end add 'as it applies both in relation to the Crown in right of Her Majesty's Government in Northern Ireland and in relation to the Crown in right of Her Majesty's Government in the United Kingdom';

(c)   in the definition of 'fire brigade' for the words from 'means' to the end substitute 'has the same meaning as in the Fire Services (Northern Ireland) Order 1984';

(d)   in the definition of 'prison officer' for the words from 'means' to the end substitute 'means any individual who holds any post, otherwise than as a medical officer, to which he has been appointed under section 2(2) of the Prison Act (Northern Ireland) 1953 or who is a prison custody officer within the meaning of Chapter III of Part VIII of the Criminal Justice and Public Order Act 1994';

(e)   in the definition of 'service for purposes of a Minister of the Crown or government department' at the end add 'or service as the head of a Northern Ireland department'.

45.   Omit section 65.

46.   For section 67 substitute—

67.   'Regulations and orders etc.

(1)   Any power under this Act to make regulations or orders shall be exercisable by statutory rule for the purposes of the Statutory Rules (Northern Ireland) Order 1979.

(2)   Any such power may be exercised to make different provision for different cases, including different provision for different areas or localities.

(3)   Any such power, includes power—

(a)   to make such incidental, supplementary, consequential or transitional provision as appears to the Northern Ireland department exercising the power to be expedient; and

(b)   to provide for a person to exercise a discretion in dealing with any matter.

(4)   No order shall be made under section 50(3) unless a draft of the order has been laid before and approved by a resolution of the Assembly.

(5)   Any other order made under this Act, other than an order under section 3(9), 52(8), 54(6) or 70(3), and any regulations made under this Act shall be subject to negative resolution within the meaning of section 41(6) of the Interpretation Act (Northern Ireland) 1954 as if they were statutory instruments within the meaning of that Act.

(6)   Section 41(3) of the Interpretation Act (Northern Ireland) 1954 shall apply in relation to any instrument or document which by virtue of this Act is required to be laid before the Assembly as if it were a statutory instrument or statutory document within the meaning of that Act.

(7)   Subsection (1) does not require an order under section 43 which applies only to a specified vehicle, or to vehicles of a specified person, to be made by statutory rule.

(8)   Nothing in section 40(6) or 46(5) affects the powers conferred by subsections (2) and (3).'

47.—(1)   For section 68(1) substitute—

'(1)   In this Act—

'accessibility certificate' means a certificate issued under section 41(1)(a);

'act' inculdes a deliberate omission;

'the Agency' means the Labour Relations Agency;

'approval certificate' means a certificate issued under section 42(4);

'the Assembly' means the Northern Ireland Assembly;

'benefits', in Part II, has the meaning given in section 4(4);

'the Department of Economic Development' means the Department of Economic Development in Northern Ireland;

'the Department of the Environment' means the Department of the Environment for Northern Ireland;

'the Department of Health and Social Services' means the Department of Health and Social Services for Northern Ireland;

'employment' means, subject to any prescribed provision, employment under a contract of service or of apprenticeship or a contract personally to do work and related expressions are to be construed accordingly;

'employment at an establishment in Northern Ireland' is to be construed in accordance with subsections (2) to (5);

'enactment' means any statutory provision within the meaning of section 1(f) of the Interpretation Act (Northern Ireland) 1954;

'government department' means a Northern Ireland department or a department of the Government of the United Kingdom;

'Minister of the Crown' includes the Treasury;

'Northern Ireland department' includes (except in sections 51 and 52) the head of a Northern Ireland department;

'occupational pension scheme' has the same meaning as in the Pension Schemes (Northern Ireland) Act 1993;

'premises', inculdes land of any description;

'prescribed' means prescribed by regulations;

'profession' includes any vocation or occupation;

'provider of services' has the meaning given in section 19(2)(b);

'public service vehicle' and 'regulated public service vehicle' have the meaning given in section 40;

'PSV accessibility regulations' means regulations made under section 40(1);

'rail vehicle' and 'regulated rail vehicle' have the meaning given in section 46;

'rail vehicle accessibility regulations' means regulations made under section 46(1);

'regulations' means—

 (a) in Parts I and II of this Act, section 66, the definition of 'employment' above and subsections (3) and (4) below, regulations made by the Department of Economic Development;

 (b) in Part V of this Act, regulations made by the Department of the Environment;

 (c) in any other provision of this Act, regulations made by the Department of Health and Social Services.

'section 6 duty' means any duty imposed by or under section 6;

'section 15 duty' means any duty imposed by or under section 15;

'section 21 duty' means any duty imposed by or under section 21;

'taxi' and 'regulated taxi' have the meaning given in section 32;

'taxi accessibility regulations' means regulations made under section 32(1);

'trade' includes any business;

'trade organisation' has the meaning given in section 13;

'vehicle examiner' means an officer of the Department of the Environment authorised by that Department for the purposes of sections 41 and 42.'.

(2) In section 68(2) to (4) for 'Great Britain' wherever it occurs substitute 'Northern Ireland'.

48.—(1) In section 70(3) for 'Secretary of State' substitute 'Department of Health and Social Services'.

(2) In section 70(8) for 'the Secretary of State' substitute 'a Northern Ireland department' and for 'him' substitute 'it'.

49.—(1) In Schedule 1 in paragraph 7(1) for 'Act 1944' substitute 'Act (Northern Ireland) 1945'.

(2)   In Schedule 1 in paragraph 7(7) for '1944' substitute '1945'.

50.—(1)   In Schedule 3 in paragraph 1—

(a)   for 'a conciliation officer' wherever it occurs substitute 'the Agency';

(b)   in sub-paragraphs (1) and (4) for 'he' substitute 'it';

(c)   in sub-paragraph (3) for 'the conciliation officer' substitute 'the Agency'.

(2)   In Schedule 3 for paragraph 4(1) substitute—

'(1)   In any proceedings under section 8—

(a)   a certificate signed by or on behalf of a Minister of the Crown or a Northern Ireland department and certifying that any conditions or requirements specified in the certificate were imposed by that Minister or that department (as the case may be) and were in operation at a time or throughout a time so specified; or

(b)   a certificate signed by or on behalf of the Secretary of State and certifying that an act specified in the certificate was done for the purpose of safeguarding national security,

shall be conclusive evidence of the matters certified.'.

(3)   In Schedule 3 in paragraph 6(1) omit 'or a sheriff court'.

(4)   In Schedule 3 for paragraph 8(1) substitute—

'(1)   In any proceedings under section 25—

(a)   a certificate signed by or on behalf of a Minister of the Crown or a Northern Ireland department and certifying that any conditions or requirements specified in the certificate were imposed by that Minister or that department (as the case may be) and were in operation at a time or throughout a time so specified; or

(b)   a certificate signed by or on behalf of the Secretary of State and certifying that an act specified in the certificate was done for the purpose of safeguarding national security,

shall be conclusive evidence of the matters certified.'.

51.—(1)   In Schedule 4 in paragraphs 2(1) and (5) and 7(1) and (5) omit 'or sisted'.

(2)   In Schedule 4 in paragraph 4 for 'Secretary of State' substitute 'Department of Economic Development'.

(3)   In Schedule 4 in paragraph 6(1) omit 'or, in Scotland, to the sheriff'.

(4)   In Schedule 4 omit paragraph 6(2).

(5)   In Schedule 4 in paragraph 9 for 'Secretary of State' substitute 'Department of Health and Social Services'.

52.—(1)   In Schedule 5 in the heading for 'National' substitute 'Northern Ireland'.

(2)   In Schedule 5 for 'Secretary of State' wherever it occurs substitute 'Department of Health and Social Services'.

(3)   In Schedule 5 in paragraphs 3(6), 5(1), 6 and 6(2) for 'he' substitute 'it' and in paragraph 3(7) for 'his' substitute 'its'.

(4)   In Schedule 5 in paragraphs 5(2) and 7(d) for 'Treasury' substitute 'Department of Finance and Personnel in Northern Ireland'.

(5)   In Schedule 5 in paragraph 8(2) for 'each House of Parliament' substitute 'the Assembly'.

53.   For Schedules 6 and 7 substitute—

'SCHEDULE 6
CONSEQUENTIAL AMENDMENTS

The Industrial Relations (Northern Ireland) Order 1976 (NI 16)

1.   In Article 68(6) of the Industrial Relations (Northern Ireland) Order 1976 (reinstatement or re-engagement of dismissed employees)—

(a)   in the definition of 'relevant complaint of dismissal', omit 'or' and at the end insert 'or a complaint under section 8 of the Disability Discrimination Act 1995 arising out of a dismissal';

(b)   in the definition of 'relevant conciliation powers', omit 'or' and at the end insert 'or paragraph 1 of Schedule 3 to the Disability Discrimination Act 1995';

(c)   in the definition of 'relevant compromise contract' for 'or Article' substitute 'Article' and at the end insert 'or section 9(2) of the Disability Discrimination Act 1995'.

The Companies (Northern Ireland) Order 1986 (NI 6)

3.   In paragraph 9 of Schedule 7 to the Companies (Northern Ireland) Order 1986 (disclosure in directors' report of company policy in relation to disabled persons) in the definition of 'disabled person' in sub-paragraph (4)(b) for 'Disabled Persons (Employment) Act (Northern Ireland) 1945' substitute 'Disability Discriminaton Act 1995'.

SCHEDULE 7
REPEALS

Chapter	Short title	Extent of repeal
1945 c. 6 (N.I.)	The Disabled Persons (Employment) Act (Northern Ireland) 1945.	Sections 1 to 4 Sections 6 to 14. In section 16 the words 'vocational training and industrial rehabilitation courses and', the words 'courses and' and the words from :'and in selecting' to 'engagement'. Section 19. Section 21. Section 22.
1960 c. 4 (N.I.)	The Disabled Persons (Employment) Act (Northern Ireland) 1960.	The whole Act.
1976 NI 16	The Industrial Relations (Northern Ireland) Order 1976.	In Article 68(6) the word 'or' in the definitions of 'relevant complaint of dismissal' and 'relevant conciliation powers'.'.

Index